FLORIDA FIREARMS

LAW, USE & OWNERSHIP

FOURTH EDITION

By: Jon H. Gutmacher, Esq.

Copyright 2001 by jon h. gutmacher

WARLORD PUBLISHING
-- a division of --
Jon H. Gutmacher, P.A.
200 N. Thornton Ave.
Orlando, Florida 32801
Phone: (407) 650-0770

www.FloridaFirearmsLaw.com

Author: Jon H. Gutmacher

First Publication: November 1993
Fourth Printing: Sept. 1997; Feb. 98; Dec. 98; Oct. 1999; Jan. 2001

Copyright 1993, 1995, 1997, 1998, 1999, & 2001 by jon h. gutmacher

Warnings & Disclaimer:

Although the author has extensively researched the materials in this book, and in the updates, to ensure accuracy, the author, publisher, distributors, and retailers specifically disclaim, and assume no liability or responsibility for its use, reliance on its content, or reliance on any update, whatsoever, nor do they assume any liability or responsibility for errors, inaccuracies, omissions, misinterpretations, or any inconsistency contained, and specifically disclaim such, as well as disclaiming any other possible liability premised upon reliance or use of this book, or any updates, including liability for negligence. This book, and any updates, are not rendered as legal advise, are the opinions of the author based upon experience and research, and should not be relied on as legal advice. For legal advise, an attorney should always be consulted regarding specific questions, and how your question relates to specific instances. This is especially true as the law is always changing. Moreover, the opinions of other attorneys, and those of the author might differ. All and any warranties, express or implied, including those for Implied Warranty of Fitness for a Particular Purpose, or Implied Warranty of Merchantability are specifically disclaimed.

This book is a copyrighted work protected under the laws of the United States of America, and no part of the book may be reproduced, in print, photocopy, electronically, on the Internet, or otherwise, without first obtaining the specific written permission of the author.

ISBN 0-9641958-2-8 $21.95

The author wishes to thank, and gratefully
acknowledge Kel-Tec for supplying
the cover photograph of its P-11 caliber 9 mm Luger
fourteen ounce, 11 shot handgun

**Cover photo: KEL-TEC P-11 Caliber 9 mm Luger
full size**

TABLE OF CONTENTS

FORWARD: ix

INTRODUCTION xi

**CHAPTER ONE: THE RIGHT TO BEAR ARMS
AND CONSTITUTIONAL ASPECTS** 1

    THE BILL OF RIGHTS 1
    A WELL REGULATED MILITIA: 1
    THE RIGHT TO KEEP AND BEAR ARMS: 3
    A WARNING ABOUT CONSTITUTIONAL
        INTERPRETATION: 3
    FLORIDA CONSTITUTIONAL RIGHT TO
        KEEP AND BEAR ARMS: 5
        ARTICLE I, SECTION 8: 5
    PREEMPTION LAW: 5
    STATISTICAL DATA ON USE OF FIREARMS: 6
    THE EXTENSION OF THE POWERS OF CONGRESS: . . 7
    A BRIEF LESSON IN CONSTITUTIONAL LAW 8
    FLORIDA CONSTITUTIONAL REVISION
        ON FIREARMS SALES: 12

**CHAPTER TWO: QUALIFICATIONS FOR PURCHASING,
        OR POSSESSION OF FIREARMS** 13

    DEFINITION OF A "FIREARM"? 13
    EXCEPTIONS TO THE DEFINITION OF "FIREARM": . 14
    ANTIQUE FIREARMS -- AND OTHER EXCEPTIONS: 14
    REQUIREMENTS TO PURCHASE FROM DEALER: . . 15
        AGE REQUIREMENTS: 15
        AGE REQUIREMENTS — NON-DEALER: 16
    REQUIREMENTS FOR UNDER 18 16
        PURCHASE ALLOWED WITH PERMISSION: . . 16
        PURCHASE DISALLOWED: 16
        USE EXCEPT UNDER ADULT SUPERVISION: 17
    YOUTH HANDGUN SAFETY AMENDMENT 17

SOME QUESTIONS ABOUT AGE: 18
RESIDENCE REQUIREMENTS: 20
    DUAL RESIDENCE: 22
    PURCHASE BY ALIENS: 23
DISABILITIES IMPOSED BY LAW: 23
PURCHASE FROM A PRIVATE INDIVIDUAL: 23
PURCHASE FROM A LICENSED FIREARMS DEALER: 25
FLORIDA FIREARMS PURCHASE PROGRAM: 26
ARREST FOR "DANGEROUS" CRIME: 27
CHART OF ARRESTS PREVENTING APPROVAL: ... 27
SOME OTHER DISABILITIES: 28
PERSON ON FLORIDA PROBATION: 28
EFFECT OF A FELONY RECORD: 29
THREE YEAR WAITING PERIOD 29
WAITING PERIOD FOR HANDGUN PURCHASES: .. 29
CHART OF PERMITTED/NON-PERMITTED SALES: . 31

CHAPTER THREE: WHAT TO DO AFTER THEY
    TURN YOU DOWN 33

THE APPROVAL (OR DISAPPROVAL) PROCESS: ... 33
IDENTIFICATION NECESSARY: 34
THE COMPUTER CHECK BY FDLE: 34
HOW THE FDLE CALL-IN SYSTEM OPERATES: 34
WHAT HAPPENS IF THE COMPUTERS ARE DOWN: . 35
PROBLEMS WITH MIS-IDENTIFICATION: 36
APPROVAL, OR NON-APPROVAL NUMBERS
    FROM FDLE: 37
APPEAL PROCEDURE & CRIMINAL
    HISTORY REVIEW: 37
A QUICK HINT: 38
THE BRADY ACT & NICS: 38

CHAPTER FOUR: REMOVAL OF LEGAL DISABILITIES . 41

EXECUTIVE CLEMENCY: 41
PARDON POWER: 41
RESTORATION OF CIVIL RIGHTS: 42
APPLICATION FOR PARDON, OR RESTORATION: 43
OUT OF STATE, AND FEDERAL CONVICTIONS: 44
AUTOMATIC GRANT OF PARTIAL RESTORATION
      OF CIVIL RIGHTS: 44
WAIVER OF RULES: 45
CASES OF EXCEPTIONAL MERIT: 45
FLORIDA INTERPRETATION ON RESTORATION: .. 45
FEDERAL PROCEDURE TO REMOVE DISABILITY: . 46

CHAPTER FIVE: FLORIDA CONCEALED WEAPONS
     PERMIT 49

QUALIFICATIONS FOR THE CONCEALED WEAPONS
      PERMIT: 49
COMPLETING THE APPLICATION PROCESS: 52
PROHIBITED PLACES WITH CONCEALED PERMIT: 53
LICENSE VIOLATIONS: 57
LOST LICENSES, OR CHANGE OF ADDRESS: 57
SUSPENSION OR REVOCATION OF YOUR PERMIT: 58
CHART OF WHY LICENSE CAN BE REVOKED: 59
HOW YOU CAN CARRY CONCEALED: 60
WHY CONCEALED PERMITS ARE THE BEST 60
RECIPROCITY OF PERMITS: 61
WARNING ABOUT DOMESTIC VIOLENCE: 61
SUMMARY AND CHART: 62
CHART — STATISTICS OF CONCEALED PERMITS: 62

CHAPTER SIX: TRANSPORTATION AND CARRYING OF WEAPONS, AND FIREARMS 63

THE LEGAL CARRYING OF FIREARMS -- LISTED: .. 63
LEGAL CARRYING AND TRANSPORTATION: 66
AUTOMOBILES AND PRIVATE VEHICLES: 66
SECURELY ENCASED 66
READILY ACCESSIBLE FOR IMMEDIATE USE 70
THE WAY IT USED TO BE 71
INTER-STATE TRANSPORTATION OF FIREARMS: .. 72
PRIVATE BOATS: 73
COMMERCIAL AIRCRAFT: 73
PRIVATE AIRCRAFT: 74
TRAINS, BUSES, AND OTHER TRANSPORTATION: . 74
CARRYING IN YOUR HOME OR BUSINESS: 75
WHEN YOU STILL CAN'T HAVE IT: 78
SCHOOLS, COLLEGES, UNIVERSITIES: 78
NATIONAL FORESTS: 78
STATE FORESTS AND PARKS 78
SENDING FIREARMS THROUGH THE MAIL: 79

CHAPTER SEVEN: COMMON WEAPONS VIOLATIONS . 81

CARRYING CONCEALED WEAPONS & FIREARMS: 81
PEPPER SPRAY, TEAR-GAS, & POCKET KNIVES: .. 82
ELECTRIC & CHEMICAL WEAPONS: 84
OPEN CARRYING OF WEAPONS: 85
IMPROPER EXHIBITION: 86
DISCHARGING FIREARMS IN PUBLIC: 87
DISCHARGING MACHINEGUNS: 87
MACHINEGUNS, UNDERSIZED FIREARMS,
    AND OTHER NFA WEAPONS: 88
CHART ON LEGAL GUN & BARREL LENGTH: 91
USING A FIREARM WHILE UNDER THE INFLUENCE: 91
SHOOTING AT VEHICLES, VESSELS
    & STRUCTURES: 92
SELF-PROPELLED KNIVES: 93
POSSESSION BY CONVICTED FELON: 93

USE/ POSSESSION WHILE COMMITTING A FELONY: 94
USE OF BULLETPROOF VEST: 95
ARMOR PIERCING OR SPECIALITY AMMUNITION: 95
ALTERED OR REMOVED SERIAL NUMBERS: 98
DESTRUCTIVE DEVICES: 98
SWITCHBLADE KNIFE: 99
ASSAULT WEAPONS: 100
USE OF BANGSTICKS 100
ARMED TRESPASS 101
LICENSED PRIVATE SECURITY GUARDS 102

CHAPTER EIGHT: LAWS CONCERNING CHILDREN . . 105

LAWFUL AGE TO POSSESS FIREARMS
        OR AMMUNITION: 105
FLORIDA LAWS PERTAINING TO MINORS 107
PENALTIES & CHART FOR CHILD VIOLATIONS: . . 108
STORAGE OF LOADED FIREARMS: 111
CIVIL PROBLEMS IF THE KIDS GET TO IT: 112
GUN FREE SCHOOL ZONES ACT -- PART TWO: . . . 113
FLORIDA SCHOOL ZONE LAWS: 114
TRAINING CHILDREN TO BE SAFE 118

CHAPTER NINE: WHAT DEALERS SHOULD KNOW . . . 121

WHO MUST SECURE A FEDERAL LICENSE: 121
WHAT DOES THE LICENSE COVER: 121
LICENSED COLLECTORS: 122
OBTAINING THE FFL: 122
DENIAL OF APPLICATION: 123
PROCEDURE ON REVOCATION OF FFL: 123
ADMINISTRATIVE REVIEW OF RECORDS
        AND INVENTORY: 124
SALE TO LEGAL ALIENS: 125
BRADY LAW REQUIREMENTS 125
SALES FROM PERSONAL COLLECTION: 126
SALE OF MULTIPLE FIREARMS: 126

THEFT OF FIREARMS 126
PAWNBROKERS: 126
SELLING TO PERSONS WITH IMPAIRMENTS: 127
SELLING TO KIDS: 128
SALE OF AMMUNITION TO MINOR 128
REQUIRED WARNING NOTICES UPON SALE: 129
STUFF YOU GOTTA SELL: 130
STUFF YOU JUST CAN'T SELL IN FLORIDA: 130
BALLISTIC, OR "SPRING" KNIVES: 131
FIREARM INSTRUCTORS: 132
FFL OPERATING OUT OF HOME: 132

CHAPTER TEN: THE ASSAULT WEAPONS BAN 133

BACKGROUND ON THE BAN: 133
GENERAL PROVISIONS OF THE BAN: 134
EXEMPTED FIREARMS: 135
CHART OF EXEMPTED TYPES OF FIREARMS: 135
SEMI-AUTOMATIC ASSAULT WEAPON: 135
UNNAMED SEMI-AUTOMATIC RIFLES: 136
UNNAMED SEMI-AUTOMATIC SHOTGUNS: 136
TRANSFER OF AN ASSAULT WEAPON, OR
        LARGE CAPACITY FEEDING DEVICE: 137
EXEMPTED FIREARMS 137
THE AFTERMATH, AND SOME ANALYSIS: 139
A QUOTE FROM HITLER ON GUN CONTROL: 140
A QUOTE FROM THOMAS JEFFERSON: 141

**CHAPTER ELEVEN: SELF DEFENSE, AND THE LAWFUL
    USE OF FORCE** 145

SOME PRACTICAL PROBLEMS OF SELF-DEFENSE: 145
FORCIBLE FELONY 146
DEADLY WEAPON: 147
IMMINENT: 148
REASONABLE BELIEF ("reasonably believes"): 148
DEADLY FORCE: 149

JUSTIFIABLE USE OF NON-DEADLY FORCE: 150
EXCESSIVE FORCE: 151
JUSTIFIABLE USE OF DEADLY FORCE: 152
DUTY TO RETREAT: 153
DEADLY FORCE -- USE TO PREVENT ESCAPE: ... 156
SOME OF THE POSSIBLE CRIMES AND PENALTIES
      FOR EXCESSIVE FORCE: 158
        MANSLAUGHTER: 158
        AGGRAVATED ASSAULT: 160
A NEEDED SELF-DEFENSE STATUTE: 161
EXCUSABLE HOMICIDE: 161
DEFENSES TO CIVIL LIABILITY (C.776.085): 163
OTHER CIVIL PROBLEMS: 163
        INSURANCE: 163
SUMMARY ON THE USE & DISPLAY OF WEAPONS 164
SELF-DEFENSE CASE EXAMPLES: 167
A SUMMARY ON SELF-DEFENSE LAW: 169
WHAT TO DO AFTER THE POLICE ARRIVE 170
911 — USE IT! 172
CELLULAR PHONES — YOUR BEST DEFENSE: ... 172
GETTING STOPPED BY THE POLICE: 173
NANOSECONDS TO REACT: 174
SENTENCING HELL 1999: 178
A NEEDED CONSTITUTIONAL AMENDMENT: 181
CONCLUSION 182

ENDNOTES: 183

ADDENDUM: 199

PRIOR EDITIONS OF "FLORIDA FIREARMS": 199
UPDATING SERVICE: 199
LIST OF SECOND AMENDMENT ORGANIZATIONS: 200

INDEX: 201

ORDERING INFORMATON 213-214
ABOUT THE AUTHOR .... back inside cover

FORWARD

I was assisting a Sergeant on a local police department range about four years ago while we were teaching a firearms safety course. During a break he handed me a book he had recently acquired, and told me it was the only up-to-date, viable work of its kind, and that it covered everything anybody would want to know about the law concerning firearms, weapons, and self-defense. He told me I should read it. I thought I didn't need to, but when I took it home, I found myself reading it three times straight, cover-to-cover. The book was an earlier version of the one you are holding: "FLORIDA FIREARMS — Law, Use & Ownership".

While reading it, I became convinced that it was the very best work of its kind I have ever seen, anywhere. The author, who I've since had the pleasure to meet, and call a friend, has relentlessly researched his data, and is considered in the trade as not just an expert on the subject, but is also known as "the man who wrote the book". But, it's not just a book about the law — it's a serious reality check on how the law actually works, and how to unravel the confusion. More importantly, it wasn't written for lawyers, it was written for you and me — and not only is it understandable, but it has humor, and is a quick read. That's really something when you realize that this is one of the most over-regulated areas of the law there is!

When I teach a course in firearms tactics for the average citizen, the fear they express isn't so much of criminal attack, instead, it's the fear of what happens afterwards. "Will the police arrest me?" "How will I pay for my defense?" "What if I get sued? Will I lose everything I own just because I defended my life, and the lives of my family?"

These are serious concerns — but most firearms instructors, including police officers, are not equipped to handle any but the most basic answers — and many times, the answers they give are dead wrong. We're not lawyers, and never will be. Why kid yourself? Even most lawyers don't deal with this stuff regularly enough to know all the nuances. So, where do we get the advice? How do we keep ourselves, and our students out of trouble?

Common sense is a good starting place, but if you don't know the rules — it's kind of tough to play the game. So, like I said before, I advise my students, my instructors, and my friends that there is only one "reliable" place to do that — and that starts and ends with reading this book.

Take the author's advice. This is the man professionals call for legal and practical guidance. This is the man I want to defend me if I ever get in a jam. Read it! Not once, not twice — but on a regular basis, because every time you pick it up you'll find something you missed the last time you looked at it. I've put a protective cover on mine, and I still wear books out on a regular basis.

There's not much more I can tell you. I've been doing this all my lifetime, and I know a good thing when I see it. If you want to stay out of jail, and keep from paying serious attorney fees on a mistake that could have been prevented — this book is the best answer you'll ever find. Tell your friends about it if they really are your friends. I do.

Gary W. Belson
Firearms Instructor

INTRODUCTION

Lots of things have changed since this book was begun back in 1993. It originally took ten months and around 2000 hours of my time to complete, and I wasn't sure if anybody would be interested in it. Thirty seven thousand copies later, this newest revision proves the continuing importance of the book. I update it almost twice a year during each reprinting. Thus, the book you are reading is a refinement of the one before, and so on. New editions are about every two years, and are substantial in nature. That's why each new "edition" gets a different color from the last, whereas updated printings retain the same color and edition number.

I began getting involved in firearms issues a few years after getting out of the State Attorney's Office. I would go to gun shows, and give out free literature on self-defense issues, because nobody knew what the heck it was all about. I used to get asked all sorts of other questions about firearms law, and had absolutely no idea what the answers were. I used to tell people I didn't know, and then would give them the answer I thought was most logical, based on my training and experience. I'd then tell them to come back the next day, and I'd look it up to make sure I had it right. The shock was — I was never right! Every time I used logic — I got the answer wrong!

I soon learned that the only way to know firearms law was to actually look up the statute, then read the other statutes that modified the first one, then read any regulations that pertained to them, and then, when I still didn't understand what the heck they were talking about, I'd read the cases that interpreted them all. Then — if it was a federal regulatory issue, I'd call up ATF Technology Branch in Washington — just to see if I got it right. With luck, I would.

What I'm trying to say is that it's no easy field, especially when you get into federal law. The law doesn't always mean what it says, and more than fifty per cent of the time it means something entirely different than what you think you've read. Moreover, the statutes are interconnected. If you don't chart them together, you will get it totally wrong! Even lawyers have a hard time with this area.

That was the reason I first started to write the book — nobody knew the <u>correct</u> answer to even some of the most basic questions. Sure, they had an answer -- but it was wrong more than half the time. Heck, even the firearm instructors I talked to didn't have the slightest idea of what the law really was, and police instructors were the worst! More alarming, these were the guys who were teaching everyone else, and they didn't really care if they were getting it right, or not. They learned the law from what somebody else told them, and from a cursory glance at the statutes. Now, there was nothing more to learn They knew it all!

They didn't care what was in my book. Didn't care what the case law said. And, for sure, no low-life, civilian attorney was gonna change their minds, or teach them anything. No way!

Frightening!

Anyway, that's how it started. Slowly, the attitude is changing, and we now have seven police academies, eighty law enforcement agencies, almost every Florida law school library, and every Florida appellate court library, including the library at the Florida Supreme Court carrying and using the book. Hopefully, they're reading it, too.

As I've said in the original introduction to the 1993 edition -- you may not like everything you read here, but you need to know it. The law is not simple, and your rights are far from what you would wish them to be, what they should be, or what the framers of the Constitution could ever have comprehended would happen. Criminals have the advantage, and the legal system is more on their side than yours. We live in a society that has largely forgotten how to defend itself, and all too often punishes those who try.

FLORIDA FIREARMS was written in response to the hundreds of questions I have answered over the past seven years -- gathered from both lecturing, researching, and promoting the book, as well as from the numerous firearms, weapons, assault, and self-defense cases I have handled as an attorney, both for the prosecution and the defense.

As with all books about the law, there is a warning that it carries.

That warning is that no matter what you do, there is no guarantee that the law will be interpreted in your favor, even when it seems clear to you. Because many of the issues have not been decided on by the courts, there was a certain amount of information that was left to my interpretation, and interpretations can be changed when an appellate court gets hold of the issue. Moreover, firearms law is a field of mountainous regulations that are always changing, and when you talk about the area of self-defense, your actions will be judged after-the-fact, by persons far removed from the actual circumstances. Common sense rarely seems to apply, and you must know what the law says in order to legally survive.

While this book is not written as legal advice, it's been found to be authorative by an awful lot of very knowledgeable people including the NRA, Florida Sheriffs Association, Florida Association of State Troopers, and the American Firearms Industry. It will clarify most of your questions about some very complicated areas, and will point out the areas of law that appear to remain in controversy. While it's not perfect -- it's by far, the best thing that's out there!

Jon H. Gutmacher, Esq.

CHAPTER ONE

THE RIGHT TO BEAR ARMS
AND CONSTITUTIONAL ASPECTS

On December 15, 1791, the Congress of the United States ratified the first ten amendments to the Constitution. These Amendments have been become known to us as the "Bill of Rights". Foremost among them, from the standpoint of this book, is Article II -- the Second Amendment.

In a historical context, the Second Amendment covers two clearly distinct concerns of the framers of our Constitution. One was to insure the rights of the People to keep and bear arms. The other was to insure the existence of the popular militia. I will discuss both.

THE BILL OF RIGHTS
ARTICLE TWO -- THE SECOND AMENDMENT

"A well regulated militia, being necessary to the security of a free State, the right of the people to keep and bear arms, shall not be infringed."

A WELL REGULATED MILITIA:

At the time of the Constitutional Convention, a loose confederation of thirteen individual colonies had just defeated King George of England in what was basically a citizen's revolution. For the most part, the American Revolution was won by a collection of locally organized militia which had been banded together into larger groups and armies to fight the common enemy, the British. These militia were comprised of freemen from all walks of life, who were locally organized, self-armed, and who trained and drilled under locally elected leaders. This was the choice method of defense -- as regular, or "standing armies" were thought by many of the free populace to be instruments of tyranny -- the means by which despots and kings were able to control their subjects by force, and thereby rule. Thus, the definition of "well regulated militia", was simply

1

a well understood reference to an independent group of self-armed freemen, under self-elected leadership, who regularly or occasionally drilled, and were not under government control. In more general terms, it was clearly understood that the phrase "well regulated militia" referred to the "body of the people", ie: the free citizens of the land, as a whole.[1]

There was much argument during the Constitutional Convention whether the creation of a central government would tend to foster tyranny, and much of this discussion revolved around the argument as to whether a standing army for this central government should be permitted, at all. Many enlightened thinkers of the time believed in the concept that "power tends to corrupt", and thus there was a basic fear of any central-ized government, and its eventual ability to oppress.

The only counter to this fear was that a well organized militia comprised of the free people of the several states would always be more powerful than any standing army -- and thus the People could overthrow any corruption of government by force of numbers. Moreover, the thinking that also pervaded the times was clearly that the local militia would always be necessary to the national and local defense -- as there was no desire to allow a centralized government to gain such power as to obviate this need. Of course, to guarantee these beliefs, the right for a people's militia had to be ensured. The result of this thinking lies in the first part of the wording in the Second Amendment: "being necessary to a free state".

Somehow, the well regulated militia has passed-away over time, and has been replaced by the professional soldier, the National Guard, and an organized police force. The National Guard has little to do with what the Framers of the Constitution envisioned as "a well regulated militia" as it lacks the localization, freedom from government control, and freedom from government purse strings that would be necessary to this concept. In fact, the National Guard would have been defined as a "select militia" in the late 1700's, that term meaning a militia armed and maintained by the government, and obviously subject to its discipline.

So, don't get thrown off track by media misinformation. A "well organized militia" historically referred to the body of the free citizens of this country, locally organized, and free of government control. While we probably don't need such active militias now, the right to have them is historic, and is guaranteed in the Constitution.

THE RIGHT TO KEEP AND BEAR ARMS:

What phrasing could be any more clear than that of "the right of the people to keep and bear arms, shall not be infringed." Yet, today, the media, many politicians, and various anti-gun organizations have so contorted the origins of this amendment, that hardly anyone except a historian understands that it means exactly what it says. Let's take it from its historical precedents.

First, you should know that the primary argument regarding this particular Constitutional provision at the Constitutional Convention was not whether the People had the right to keep and bear arms -- but that this particular right was so fundamental that it was almost tantamount to an insult to have to put it in writing, and include it. It was an "inalienable" right. A "natural" right. A "personal" right. Something about which there could be no reasonable debate.

The natural or inalienable portion of the right was tied to the right of self-defense, a right which was believed to be so inherent to the individual that no government could legitimately curtail it.   The mere thought that government could infringe upon this right was anathema.

Thus, the right to keep and bear arms was just that -- that every freeman had the right to have weapons, and use them in his own defense. It was not tied to a "well regulated militia". In fact, a clause to add a phrase that the right was "for the common defense" -- was soundly rejected by the Constitutional Convention, just for that reason.[2]

Don't let anybody tell you differently!

A WARNING ABOUT CONSTITUTIONAL INTERPRETATION:

People should be wary about constitutional changes. Everytime the State or Federal Constitution is amended -- you, the ordinary citizen, are giving-up more and more of your "retained", and supposedly "inalienable" rights.

Why?

Because in our country, government derives <u>all</u> of its power from the People. This is in the form of those grants of power embodied in the Constitution. What the Constitution says the government can do -- is all it is authorized to do, nothing more! If it wasn't given to the government in the constitution -- it is "retained" by the People -- and the government cannot legally interfere with any of these "retained" rights.

So, why do we have a "Bill of Rights"? Aren't these rights retained, anyway?

Basically, whenever a Bill of Rights is adopted, it is a precaution-ary statement of those rights which the People want to make especially sure the government realizes are off limits to legislative or judicial erosion! In other words, it's a statement by a bunch of real nervous people that don't trust the government, in the first place. Or, like Thomas Jefferson said:

"Government is a necessary evil"

In Florida we've gotten into some bad habits, because we tend to randomly amend the State Constitution on fairly regular basis, instead of recognizing it for what it is. Since a constitution is supposed to be a basic framework for government -- it's not a good idea to go amending it every year. That's what the legislature is for. They pass laws, amend laws, repeal laws -- all within the framework the constitution has set forth.

It may seem like a good idea to amend the Constitution in the heat of the moment, but most of the time, we realize we'd have been better off if we just left it alone, and let the courts or the legislature deal with it. An example of this are the additions recently made to the Florida Constitution regarding the right to keep and bear arms. Here it is:

FLORIDA CONSTITUTIONAL RIGHT TO KEEP AND BEAR ARMS:

ARTICLE I, SECTION 8:

(a)   The right of the people to keep and bear arms in defense of themselves and of the lawful authority of the state shall not be infringed, except that the manner of bearing arms may be regulated by law.

(b)   There shall be a mandatory period of three days, excluding weekends and legal holidays, between the purchase and delivery at retail of any handgun. For the purposes of this section, "purchase" means the transfer of money or other valuable consideration to the retailer and "handgun" means a firearm capable of being carried and used by one hand, such as a pistol or revolver. Holders of a concealed weapon permit as prescribed in Florida law shall not be subject to the provision of this paragraph.

(c)   The legislature shall enact legislation implementing subsection (b) of this section, effective no later than December 31, 1991, which shall provide that anyone violating the provisions of subsection (b) shall be guilty of a felony.

(d)   This restriction shall not apply to a trade in of another handgun.

The restrictions set forth in this section of the Constitution cannot be changed by the Legislature, the Governor, or the Judiciary. The People voted for it, and made it part of the "unchangeable" portion of our basic law. For better or worse, it's there forever -- unless the citizens vote to change the Constitution, again.

PREEMPTION LAW:

Florida is a "preemption" state. That means that the legislature has decided to keep local government out of firearms regulation, unless it specifically authorizes an exemption. The reason we have a preemption law is because of all the problems we had before this law was enacted. Every local government had its own version of the law, and nobody knew what the heck the law was from city-to-city, or county-to-county. In essence, it was politics at its worse — and the citizens paid the price.

F.S. 790.33 sets forth the preemption law as follows:

"Except as expressly provided by general law, the legislature hereby declares that it is occupying the whole field of regulation of firearms and ammunition, including the purchase, sale, transfer, taxation, manufacture, ownership, possession, and transportation thereof, to the exclusion of all existing and future county, city, town, or municipal ordinances or regulations relating thereto. Any such existing ordinances are hereby declared null and void. This subsection shall not affect zoning ordinances which encompass firearms businesses along with other businesses. Zoning ordinances which are designed for the purpose of restricting or prohibiting the sale, purchase, transfer, or manufacture of firearms or ammunition as a method of regulating firearms or ammunition are in conflict with this subsection and are prohibited."

. . . .

"It is the policy and intent of this section to provide uniform firearms laws in the state; to declare all ordinances and regulations null and void which have been enacted by any jurisdiction other than state and federal, which regulate firearms, ammunition, or components thereof unless specifically authorized by this section or general law; and to require local jurisdictions to enforce state firearms laws."

You might note that the preemption statute does not apply to weapons other than firearms and ammunition. This was a serious oversight by the legislature. However, under Florida constitutional law, local government is still restricted on regulating other weapons if they pass laws that conflict with C. 790.[3]

STATISTICAL DATA ON USE OF FIREARMS:

In recent years there has been a serious attempt to discredit the private ownership of firearms, and to minimize and distort the meaning of the Second Amendment. Media has taken an increasingly active part in this conspiracy, and is the leading proponent in the battle to despoil your right of self-defense, and individual freedoms. The classic argument is that if by banning firearms we can "save one life" -- it will be worth it all.[4] Of course, that means giving up more of your fast disappearing personal liberty. But more importantly, it distorts the actual truth.

Statistics compiled by the government show that firearm accidents have significantly declined over the years, not just percentage wise -- but also numerically. In fact, according to a 1990 study by the Florida Office of Vital Statistics -- Floridians are more likely to die from an accident involving medical malpractice (126), a fall (620), a drowning (453), electrocution (45), etc. than from a firearm (36).

Moreover, research done by Florida State University professor Gary Kleck has established that 800,000 to 2.5 million people a year use a firearm throughout the United States in lawful self-defense, and in stopping the commission of serious felonies.[5] How many lives are saved by firearms? Plenty! But, don't ask the media to tell you about that. That's not what they're in business for.

In an ideal society, there would be no criminals, no terrorists, no foreign enemies, and no need for self-defense. But that society is a dream, and the reality is that law-abiding citizens need a method to defend themselves, their property, and their families. A firearm furnishes that method, and if a person learns gun safety, and has a basic knowledge of what he or she can lawfully do, all of society benefits by their being armed. That is one of the basic pillars upon which this Great Nation was founded. The media be damned.

THE EXTENSION OF THE POWERS OF CONGRESS:

Earlier in this chapter I briefly mentioned why you need to be cautious about giving away your "retained rights", by constitutional amendment. Let me show you how this has run amuck in the federal system -- so you can understand where all these federal regulations are coming from, at least, from a legal standpoint.

Article 1, section 1, of the United States Constitution states that "all legislative Powers herein granted shall be vested in a Congress of the United States . . . ." That literally means that if the Constitution doesn't grant them the power -- the don't have the power. The Bill of Rights, in the Tenth Amendment, states that "the powers not delegated to the United States by the Constitution, nor prohibited by it to the States, are reserved to the States respectively, or to the people." That section basically means the same thing, but more forcefully. Literally, it means that the powers not granted to Congress, and not withheld from the states (such as the right to make treaties, formulate currency, etc.) are reserved to the several states, or their citizens.

Last but not least, we have the Ninth Amendment to the United States Constitution. This states that "the enumeration in the Constitution of certain rights, shall not be construed to deny or disparage others retained by the people". This means that those rights which were thought by the framers of the Constitutional to be the "natural" or "inalienable" rights of free citizens -- cannot be infringed upon by the government.

Well, it all sounds good, but in actuality it hasn't been working too well since the time the Civil War began. Let me show you why, by giving you a brief lesson in Constitutional law:

A BRIEF LESSON IN CONSTITUTIONAL LAW:

The Tenth Amendment to the United States Constitution reserves all powers not otherwise delegated to Congress, to the individual States, or to the People. However, Congress, with the apathetic assistance of the federal judiciary, has managed to completely usurp the purpose of this Amendment. In essence, the federal judicial system has generally failed in its responsibilities, and lets Congress run amuck by not policing it. Let me give you an example:

An extremely important federal appellate decision, United States v. Lopez, invalidated a portion of the 1990 "Gun-Free School Zones Act". This remarkably dumb federal law made it a federal felony to possess a firearm within 1000 feet of a school zone. It was dumb because if you happened to be driving within 999.9 feet of a one room wooden kindergarten, even if the kids were home on vacation, even if you didn't know it was there until you went around that blind curve in the road that suddenly revealed it, and even if there's a raging river between the road you're on and the school -- you're in deep buffalo chips with the law.

Now, you ask: "How can Congress legislate such a law? Isn't this a purely an area of state concern, reserved to the state legislatures?"

Excellent question! I see I've gotten you thinking!

However, and unfortunately, the answer, according to your wonderful federal government, is "no" -- and that's because Congress can presumably pass any law they want, under the power of the "Commerce Clause", because Congress has the Constitutionally granted power to regulate anything that "substantially affects interstate or foreign commerce", and in such instances, the Tenth Amendment doesn't apply. In other words, the Tenth Amendment would restrict the exercise of federal lawmaking jurisdiction only when there are no other clauses in the Constitution under which the Congress has power to act! In essence, this would require a process of elimination. Thus, if Congress can't pass legislation under the Commerce Clause -- is there another clause they could still pass it under? If not -- the law would be outside of its power to act, and therefore "reserved" to the States.

"Is this really the law," you ask?

The unfortunate answer is "yes" -- but that's not the most unfortunate part. You see -- the courts are supposed to have the authority to make sure that any power exercised by Congress is exercised legitimately. That's what our Founding Fathers meant by "a system of checks and balances". In other words, if the Congress wants to legislate something under the Commerce Clause, then the problem its attempting to address and rectify should, in actuality, "substantially affect interstate or foreign commerce". If it doesn't -- then it's an illegitimate use of power that's supposed to be reserved to the individual state legislatures, or the People.

The problem here is that the federal courts normally don't do that kind of policing. In actuality, they routinely "defer" to any factual findings made by Congress, no matter how unsupported, or outlandish these findings may be! All you need is some Senator or Congressman saying: "We're passing this legislation because gun possession around a school affects interstate commerce" -- and Whoop-de-Doo -- the court usually says: "Fine -- sounds good to us!"

That's basically what <u>United States v. Lopez</u> said. In fact, the Opinion of the Court actually said that it was not really its job to second guess Congress -- but, it was <u>up to the People</u> to elect representatives who would not pass unconstitutional laws under the guise of constitutional ones. To put it another way: if you elect representatives who don't understand or care about the Constitution, and your rights -- you get what you deserve.

So much for the system of "checks and balances" that our Founding Fathers envisioned. Let one part fail, and the result is that Liberty pays the price!

However, the <u>Lopez</u> court still invalidated the law because the federalists in Congress actually <u>forgot</u> to include any statement that commerce "was affected" by guns near schools when they passed the Act -- and thus the court was free to determine from a standpoint of common sense (something little used in government) -- that this stupid law really had nothing to do with interstate commerce in the first place, didn't affect it one iota -- and was therefore unconstitutional.

So, for a short time, the citizens lucked out -- only because of a simple oversight. If not, the magic words, "affecting commerce" would have been uttered at the right moment in Congress, and another oppressive law would have stayed on the books, unchecked by the one branch of government that the Founding Fathers thought would stop such abuses.

It seems that the federal courts are too political, and too "politically correct". If the Constitution must suffer -- it usually does. However, there is some rare good news in this rather one-sided area. In the last few years we've started to see changes in the cases coming out of the United States Supreme Court. It appears that a small majority of the Supreme Court is beginning to interpret legislation in a more traditional manner, consistent with our basic constitutional precepts. This is a very welcome change. In fact, in the <u>Lopez</u>[6] case that I just discussed, the Supreme Court, by a very narrow margin, sustained the decision of the federal appellate court, and agreed that the "1000 foot law" had no substantial affect on interstate commerce, and was therefore beyond the power of Congress to enact.

Of course, Congress was not to be deterred, and after the Supreme Court made it clear that the law was an unconstitutional intrusion into an area of purely state concern — Congress reenacted the law, once again, with the following findings:

"The Congress finds and declares that crime, particularly crime involving drugs and guns, is a pervasive, nationwide problem; crime at the local level is exacerbated by the interstate movement of drugs, guns, and criminal gangs; firearms and ammunition move easily in interstate commerce and have been found in increasing numbers in and around schools, as documented in numerous hearings in both the Committee on the Judiciary of the House of Representatives and the Committee on the Judiciary of the Senate; in fact, even before the sale of a firearm, the gun, its component parts, ammunition, and the raw materials from which they are made have considerably moved in interstate commerce; while criminals freely move from State to State, ordinary citizens and foreign visitors may fear to travel to or through certain parts of the country due to concern about violent crime and gun violence, and parents may decline to send their children to school for the same reason; the occurrence of violent crime in school zones has resulted in a decline in the quality of education in our country; this decline in the quality of education has an adverse impact on interstate commerce and the foreign commerce of the United States; States, localities, and school systems find it almost impossible to handle gun-related crime by themselves--even States, localities, and school systems that have made strong efforts to prevent, detect, and punish gun-related crime find their efforts unavailing due in part to the failure or inability of other States or localities to take strong measures; and the Congress has the power, under the interstate commerce clause and other provisions of the Constitution, to enact measures to ensure the integrity and safety of the Nation's schools by enactment of this subsection.

So, we're back where we started — and we've proven what we knew all along -- that Congress doesn't care about the Constitution. The question that remains now is -- since the Supreme Court has already decided that the law does not substantially affect interstate commerce — will other federal courts continue to hold the law unconstitutional -- or will they defer to the new "factual finding" Congress made in `reenacting` it?

Obviously, only the Supreme Court should be able to change that interpretation of unconstitutionality. However, federal courts tend to rule in favor of the government almost all the time. They rarely interpret the law to protect the People — instead, they interpret the law to protect the government. Again, a concept that the Founding Fathers might have trouble with. Only time will tell.

Some other recent decisions of the Supreme Court have also been promising. The Court invalidated portions of the Brady law [7], and in another case required the government to prove "willful" violations of certain firearm laws before a conviction could be obtained.[8] Still, these decisions have been won by a one vote majority -- and are being made by a very divided Court. The tide may be beginning to change, but it sure has a long way to go.

Interesting, huh?

So, now that you've gotten your first lesson in Constitutional Law, maybe you'll see the reality of how important it is in voting the right people in (or out) of office. And maybe, when next you hear someone complain, you can tell them that if things go badly, it's probably their own damn fault for not electing patriots.

CONSTITUTIONAL REVISION ON FIREARMS SALES:

The voters passed an amendment to the Florida Constitution in November 1998, which will be Article 8, section 5. It authorizes each individual county to enact ordinances, without voter approval, to require a criminal history records check as part of the sale of any firearm, private or dealer — if "any part" of the sale takes place on public property. It also authorizes each county to enact ordinances placing a 3-5 day waiting period on any such sale. The purpose of the amendment was to curtail private sales of firearms at gun shows, since Miami and Tampa were unhappy with the use of their convention centers for these purposes. The amendment will not affect private sales not made on public property, and will not affect anyone purchasing with a concealed weapons permit. Those individuals are exempted. The amendment could have been adopted as a simple statute passed by the Legislature, but since it made no real sense — the Legislature wanted no part of it. However, clever advertising, and a lack of information on the real purpose of the amendment resulted in a runaway vote for its passage.

CHAPTER TWO

QUALIFICATIONS FOR PURCHASING, OR POSSESSION OF FIREARMS

Did you notice the title of this chapter? Did it seem a little unusual? Qualifications for purchasing -- or possession of firearms? Surely, it should say qualifications for purchasing, and possession of firearms?

However, the answer is a definite no. Anytime a person seeks to purchase, borrow, own, or possess a firearm, a different set of rules probably applies. Moreover, these rules are governed by both State and Federal law. You must comply with both sets of law to be legal.

In fact, there are certain qualifications for ownership of a firearm, that are dramatically different from those required to purchase a firearm. This chapter will outline those requirements for you, at least as required by Florida and federal law. In another state, different rules could apply.

DEFINITION OF A "FIREARM"?

Before we get into the guts of this chapter, you need to know what is, and what is not -- a firearm. So, let me tell you what the definitions and non-definition of a firearm are.

In its most basic form, a firearm is any weapon that discharges a projectile by use of an explosive charge, or is designed or is readily convertible to such a use. Federal law has expanded the definition to include the frame or receiver of any such weapon, and any firearm muffler or silencer. Firearm mufflers and silencers are generally illegal, and will be covered elsewhere in this book.

The federal definition also encompasses any **"destructive devices"** which include all explosives, poison gas, bombs, grenades, rockets with more than 4 ounces of propellant, missiles with an explosive or incendiary

13

charge of over one quarter ounce, mines, and most devices which are not shotguns that have a inside barrel diameter (bore) of one half inch or more, and will fire a projectile. The definition also includes any combination of parts by which such a device can be readily assembled.

The only exception to the definition is when the item is not generally considered to be a "weapon". One such example would be a "potato cannon", which is generally considered to be a recreational device made of PVC irrigation pipe that is used to fire potatoes or golf balls by use of a propellant such as ignited hair spray or MAPP gas. Since its use is really not as a weapon -- it is not considered a "destructive device". However, if you used it as a weapon -- then it should qualify for the definition, and could get you in some very serious problems. Another example would be legal fireworks, and probably illegal fireworks, to the extent they are not being used as a weapon, but are being used merely as fireworks.[9]

EXCEPTIONS TO THE DEFINITION OF A "FIREARM":

ANTIQUE FIREARMS -- AND OTHER EXCEPTIONS:

One of the exceptions to the usual definition of a firearm is the class of weapons known as "antique firearms." An antique firearm is usually, but not always, a black-powder gun of some sort, and is generally classified as a "weapon", rather than as a "firearm". This is a major distinction in definition, because weapons that are not "firearms" escape a large number of state and federal regulations that otherwise would apply.

In order to be an "antique firearm" under Florida law, the weapon must have been manufactured during or before 1918, or be a replica of such, and it may not use "fixed ammunition" unless this fixed ammunition is no longer manufactured in the United States, and is not readily available in ordinary commerce. Under federal law the definition is basically the same, except that the year of manufacture or replica thereof is 1898. "Fixed ammunition" is defined as self-contained ammunition consisting of a case, primer, explosive charge, and projectile. However, you should be aware that if you use an antique firearm in the commission of a crime -- it becomes a firearm.[10]

Also excluded from the definition of a firearm are starter pistols that are not capable of discharging any projectile, air guns, BB guns, and pyrotechnic devices that are used for signaling, or throwing safety lines. However, case law makes it clear that a starter gun can be classified as a firearm if it is "readily convertible" to the firing of a projectile.   On the other hand, air guns and BB guns are not considered to be firearms since they don't expel a projectile by use of an explosive, although they can be defined as a weapon, or even "deadly weapon", depending upon their use, or intended use.[11]

REQUIREMENTS TO PURCHASE FROM A FIREARMS DEALER:

AGE REQUIREMENTS:

Now that you know what a firearm is, you probably want to know some of the requirements for purchasing one.   In Florida, the age of majority (ie: not a "minor") is 18 years unless otherwise specified by the Florida Constitution, or state beverage laws.   For our purposes -- that means 18 years of age, or older.

However, in order to purchase a handgun from a federal licensee (ie: a licensed firearms dealer) -- you need to be at least 21 years of age. On the other hand, in order to purchase a rifle or shotgun from a federal licensee -- you need to be at least 18 years of age.   The same age requirements apply to the purchase of ammunition for these firearms from a federal licensee. In other words, you can't buy .38 caliber ammunition from a federal licensee until you are 21 years of age, because it's not generally used in anything but a handgun. On the other hand, if you were 18 years of age, and wanted to buy .22 caliber ammunition -- if you represented it was for a rifle, it would be legal.   If you represented it was for a handgun, it would be illegal. That's because .22 caliber is used in both types of firearms. However, if you misrepresented it's use, and really wanted it for a handgun -- you'd be committing a federal felony.

If you present falsified identification, or lie on an application to obtain a firearm -- you have just committed a federal crime, as well as a third degree felony in Florida.[12] You could actually be prosecuted in both state and federal court, at the same time. If you are lucky enough to have the feds prosecute you, remember that federal prisons have lots of room. You will stay there for a long time.

AGE REQUIREMENTS -- obtaining firearm from non-dealer

Both Florida and Federal laws are primarily aimed at sales made by licensed firearms dealers to private citizens. This leaves a few loopholes when the sale is strictly between private persons, or if the transfer of a firearm is a gift between private individuals, and no licensed dealer is involved. Under Florida and Federal law, any citizen of the age of 18 years, or more, who is not under some other legal disability, may possess or own a handgun, rifle, or shotgun.

In other words -- even if it would be illegal to purchase a handgun from a licensed firearms dealer because you're not yet 21 -- it may still be legal for you to purchase, or receive it privately -- as long as you're at least 18 years of age, or older, and suffer no other legal disqualification.

REQUIREMENTS FOR UNDER 18 AND 16 YEARS OF AGE:

PURCHASE ALLOWED WITH PERMISSION:

In Florida, it is a first degree misdemeanor to give, lend, or sell a person under the age of 18 years any type of weapon (not just firearms) -- except an ordinary pocketknife, unless they are given permission to do so by one of the minor's parents, or by the minor's guardian.[13] If it's a firearm, then it's a felony. This proscription is primarily directed to private persons, since the penalty is greater for federal licensees, and other dealers.[14] Moreover, federally licensed firearms dealers cannot sell a "firearm" to anyone unless that person meets the federal age requirements of 18 or 21 years, regardless of whose permission they have.

PURCHASE DISALLOWED, EVEN WITH PERMISSION:

It is also illegal for any person who deals in weapons (any type of weapons -- not just federally licensed firearms dealers) to sell a dirk,[15] Bowie knife, brass knuckles,[16] electric weapon, or slungshot (ie: a flexible handled weapon with a weight on the end used for striking) to anyone UNDER the age of 18 years -- even with their parents permission. However, it is legal for the parent to purchase the weapon, and then give it to the child as a gift.

USE DISALLOWED EXCEPT UNDER ADULT SUPERVISION:

Furthermore, it is illegal for any child under the age of 16 years of age to use any firearm, BB gun, or electric weapon except under the attending supervision of an adult, who is acting with permission of a parent. If an adult who is then responsible for the child knows that the child is in possession of an air gun, or electric weapon in violation of this section -- then that adult is guilty of a second degree misdemeanor. A firearm is a felony -- and will probably be civilly liable for any damages caused by the minor, as well.[17] F.S. 790.22

In addition, Florida has made it a felony for an adult who is responsible for the child to knowingly and willfully permit a child under the age of 18 years to possess any firearm at any place other than the child's home, unless the following criteria are met:[18]

a. The child is engaged in lawful hunting, and is at least 16 years of age, or if under the age of 16, is being supervised by an adult while engaged in lawful hunting.

b. The child is engaged in lawful shooting competition, or practice, or other lawful recreational shooting activity, and is at least 16 years of age, or if under the age of 16, is being supervised by an adult who is acting with the consent of the minor's parent or guardian.

c. The firearm is unloaded, and is being transported directly to or from the event authorized in either (a) or (b).

Moreover, if the firearm is being kept by the child at home, it must be unloaded. Under federal law, the child could not keep a handgun in his possession at home, even if unloaded. He could only have a rifle or shotgun.[19] We'll discuss this in the next section.

YOUTH HANDGUN SAFETY AMENDMENT:

The 1994 Crime Bill passed by the United States Congress, section 110201, now codified in 18 USC 922(x), add some additional restrictions for minors (ie: under 18 years) in possession of handguns, or handgun ammunition, which somewhat overlap the Florida statute. These additional restrictions require that the minor have the prior written consent of a parent or guardian, that the written consent be kept on the minor's person at all times that he is in possession of a handgun, and that the handgun be transported unloaded and in a locked case directly to and from any lawfully enumerated activity if being transported by the minor. Remember, the restrictions here apply to handguns -- not shotguns or rifles.

It should be noted that the Florida statute does NOT permit a minor to use or possess a firearm (handgun or long gun) in the course of employment, or during ranching or farming -- whereas the federal statute does. In case you're curious about the apparent conflict, the Florida statute controls because it's more restrictive. Whether it's constitutional or not, is another question.

SOME QUESTIONS ABOUT AGE:

QUESTION: I wanted to give my nephew a really great gift on his 16th birthday, so I bought him a bow and arrows. I didn't ask his folks if I could do this because I thought they might be mad. Could I get in trouble?

ANSWER: Sure! If Mom and Dad wanted to make an issue of it, you just committed a first degree misde-meanor[20] -- because you didn't have their permis-sion to give it to the kid. On the other hand, if his Dad said it was OK -- and his Mom didn't -- you'd still be legal, although, you probably wouldn't be invited over for dinner anymore. The same thing would apply to an air gun, most knives, sword, electric weapon, mace, etc. If the kid is under 18 years of age -- you need the permission of a parent, or guardian.

QUESTION: I am a licensed firearms dealer. An 18 year old wanted to buy ammunition for his rifle, which was of a caliber that could also be used in a handgun. Can I legally sell it to him?

ANSWER: Sure. As long as he represents it's for a longgun (rifle or shotgun), and you have no real reason to doubt he's telling the truth -- you can freely do so. Obviously, the type of ammunition must be typical for the weapon he says it's for -- otherwise you're on notice that the sale could be illegal.

QUESTION: I'm only 19 years old, but I really want a handgun. My father said I could get one if I maintained at least a "B" average in school -- and I have. How do I purchase the gun?

ANSWER: As long as you are 18 years of age or older, you may legally purchase a handgun from a private owner. You do not need your parents permission. You may receive it as a gift. There may be a problem with having somebody else buy it for you from a licensed firearms dealer, although you could receive it as a gift.[21]

QUESTION: I am not a licensed firearms dealer, but I have a store, and carry a selection of knives. A juvenile and his uncle came in last week, and the uncle wanted to buy a bowie knife for his nephew. He gave the nephew the money, who handed it to me. I refused the sale. Was I right?

ANSWER: Absolutely. Otherwise, you would have committed a second degree felony. You could not sell the knife directly to the minor, even if he had been there with a parent, rather than the uncle -- since a direct sale is prohibited. You could have sold it to the uncle, even if you knew he was going to give it to his nephew -- although that might not be wise from a civil liability standpoint if there was any hint that it was without parental approval. And, of course, if the uncle then gave it to his nephew without the actual permission of a parent -- he would have committed a first degree misdemeanor, although you should be legally O.K.

RESIDENCE REQUIREMENTS:

Federal law strictly prohibits the transfer or receipt of any firearm to a non-resident by a non-licensee, and also restricts many transfers by a licensed firearms dealer to a non-licensee. It is therefore a federal crime for an ordinary citizen to sell, transfer, give, or receive a firearm when the person receiving the handgun is not a genuine resident of the state in which the transfer is made. In such instances, anyone willfully involved would be guilty of a federal felony.[22] There are a few exceptions which we will discuss, shortly.

These restriction also apply to transfers made by a federal licensee to a person who does not reside in the dealers state. However, there are again, some exceptions.

One of the exceptions occurs when the transfer is a temporary one, in the sense of a loan or rental[23] of a firearm. However, the loan is restricted to only those instances which are for a lawful sporting purpose.[24] This exception applies to both dealers, and private individuals. But, don't try to get cute with the "temporary" nature of the transfer. It's not something to play with.

Another exception is where the transfer is the result of a bequest or devise, due to the death of the owner of the firearm. In this case, a non-resident may receive the firearm bequeathed to him, regardless of his state of residence, although he still may not transport it into his residence state, unless it is legal to have it there.[25]

Rifles and shotguns are treated somewhat differently from handguns, and federal law does not prevent a qualified citizen who resides in another state from purchasing a rifle or shotgun in a face-to-face transaction with a federally licensed firearms dealer outside his state if: the purchase would be legal in both states, and if the regulatory requirements of both states are complied with.

Again, this applies only to a purchase from a licensed dealer. A private individual could not make such a sale, or transfer under any circumstance. In fact, this also applies to the gift of a gun. In other words -- if you are from out-of-state, you cannot buy or obtain a legal firearm from anyone but a licensed dealer.

What about a handgun?

Well, there's also a method by which you can buy a handgun or longgun[26] from a federally licensed dealer in another state if:

a.   The out-of-state dealer transfers the firearm to a licensed firearms dealer in your state, and

b.   So long as the receiving dealer has a copy of the license of the dealer who is sending it, and

c.   So long as the laws of both states are fully complied with, and

d.   So long as a Form 4473 is completed when you pick the firearm up.

Then, and only then may the dealer in your residence state legally transfer it to you.[27]

In Florida, one of the requirements of a sale is that a purchaser, other than another federal firearms licensee, must pass the FDLE records check, and must fill out the Form 4473 before the dealer can transfer the firearm.[28] This might cause some problems for the dealer if the firearm were a handgun being shipped out-of-state, because the records would look like he was making an in-state transfer of a handgun to a non-resident. Something very illegal.

If the records look this way, the dealer is going to have a lot of explaining to do when ATF checks his books, even though the transfer was totally legal. In retrospect, this Florida law probably wasn't meant to apply to a sale that was not being delivered in this state, but was instead being transferred out-of-state, from dealer to dealer, in conformity with federal law -- but then, who knows? Nobody has bothered to interpret it, and that's just my opinion of what would happen in a test case.

Whatever, the lesson to be learned is that you obviously can't give an out-of-state resident a firearm as a gift, unless it's delivered to him by a federal licensee in his home state.[29] And, if you want to obtain firearms from out-of-state, you'd better make sure you buy them from a federally licensed dealer, who ships them to a federally licensed dealer in your home state for your eventual pick-up.

As an additional word of warning, you should know that it is illegal for a third person to purchase a firearm with the intent of transferring it to a non-resident, or to someone who has a legal disqualification. This is known as a "straw man" purchase, and is a federal felony for anyone involved. Thus, if the dealer has reasonable cause to suspect that this is the intent of the purchaser, he cannot make the sale without committing a federal crime.

For instance. Your nephew from New Jersey comes down to Florida for a visit. He is staying with you, is over 21 years of age, has never been arrested, and is an all-around wonderful person. He knows you have a couple of handguns, and that you even have a Florida Concealed Weapons Permit. You've taken him out shooting with you at the range -- and he's a better shot than you. He's always wanted a handgun, but New Jersey law won't let him get one. He asks you if you can buy him one, and he'll pay you back. You say "sure".

You've heard it's illegal to purchase a handgun for somebody else who lives out of state, and your gun dealer tells you "no way" will he sell you one -- even if you promise to swear that it was only for you. So, you decide to give your old 38 caliber revolver to the nephew as a gift.

"What's the harm?"

The harm is that you just violated the Gun Control Act of 1968, and are subject to five years imprisonment in a federal penitentiary, and a fine of up to $5,000.00. Your nephew is also subject to the same penalty. What a great uncle, you are! Won't the family be pleased?

DUAL RESIDENCE:

It is possible for a person to have a dual residence, and thus be able to purchase a longgun or handgun in more than one state legally. This means that the state you are attempting to purchase the firearm in is not a place that you are merely visiting -- but is one in which you regularly reside, and maintain as your home. Examples would be a college student living away from home part of the year. Persons who owned permanent homes, or leased apartments in different cities where they regularly lived or worked. And people who kept permanent vacation homes where they resided part of the year. Mere ownership of property does not constitute residence. Of course, to prove residence you are probably going to have to have a driver's license from both states, or at least a state issued photographic identification card. Otherwise, most dealers would be wise not to make the sale to you.

PURCHASE BY ALIENS:

According to federal law, an alien (ie: citizens from another country -- not from another planet), other than those with a nonimmigrant visa, may purchase a firearm if they are legally in the United States, are a resident of the State in which the firearm is purchased, and have been a resident of that State for an uninterrupted " ninety continuous days". The old practice of allowing an alien to purchase a firearm by virtue of a letter from his consulate or embassy was eliminated in April 1997. The "90 continuous days" requirement means that if the alien has lived in Florida for 89 days, and goes to New York for a day -- he starts the 90 day period anew when he returns to Florida because he broke the 90 day residency requirement one day too soon. Had he left on the 91st day, and then returned -- he'd have been fine. The dealer who sells an alien a firearm must obtain proof of residency by examination of documents such as a lease showing that at least 90 days has expired since it's effective date, utility bills, or similar type proof. The proof must be noted on the Form 4473 by the dealer. Photo identification must also be presented, and documented on the Form 4473. See, 27 CFR 178.124 & 178.125. If it appears that the firearm is going to be taken out of the country, the alien must notify the Office of Munitions Control, and obtain a DSP Form 5, in order to export it. Nonimmigrant visas generally can't purchase.

DISABILITIES IMPOSED BY LAW:

PURCHASE FROM A PRIVATE INDIVIDUAL:

If you're purchasing from a private individual, you already know that you must be a resident of the same state where the purchase was made, and be at least 18 years of age. Another requirement is that you don't have a felony conviction somewhere in your past, unless this legal disability was lifted. How you get rid of a prior felony conviction is discussed later in this book.

A felony conviction means that you were convicted of a crime where the possible punishment exceeded 1 year in jail (366 days qualifies) -- whether you received this sentence or not. The determining factor is the possible punishment, and not what you got.

Under Florida law, a "withheld adjudication" does not constitute a "conviction" of a felony for most firearms purposes. Not all states follow that rule, but that's how Florida works. Lucky you! If you have a federal, or out-of-state conviction, the federal law, or laws of the state of conviction control your legal status to possess a firearm -- not Florida law.

On the other hand, if you were "adjudicated" or "convicted" under a Florida felony -- you're obviously going to have to read the upcoming chapter on removal of legal disabilities. Tough luck!

Other disabilities which would make it a crime to sell, transfer, possess, or receive the firearm include:

a.   The purchaser is under Indictment or Information for a felony, or crime punishable by more than a year in jail.

b.   The purchaser is a fugitive from justice (ie: any person who has deliberately fled another state to avoid prosecution for a crime, or avoid testifying in a criminal proceeding).

c.   The purchaser is an unlawful user, or addicted to illegal drugs (21 USC 802) (Yeah -- if you occasionally smoke marijuana -- you're illegal).

d.   The purchaser has been adjudicated a mental defective, or has been committed to any mental institution, anytime.

e.   The purchaser was dishonorably discharged.

f.   The purchaser renounced his/her U.S. citizenship.

g.   The purchaser is subject to a court order restraining the purchaser from harassing, stalking, or threatening an intimate partner[30], or child of such, or engaging in other conduct that would place the intimate partner in reasonable fear of bodily harm to the partner or child -- so long as such order was issued after a hearing of which the purchaser received actual notice, and had an opportunity to participate -- whether or not the purchaser did participate. And, the court must find that the person represented a credible threat to the physical safety of the other, or alternatively, that the court order expressly prohibits the use, threatened or attempted use of physical force.[31]

h.   The person was convicted of a crime of misdemeanor "domestic violence". A misdemeanor crime of domestic violence means an offense that has, as an element, the use or attempted use of physical force, or the threatened use of a deadly weapon, committed by a current or former spouse, parent, or guardian of the victim, by a person with whom the victim shares a child in common, by a person who is cohabiting with or has cohabited with the victim as a spouse, parent, or guardian, or by a person similarly situated to a spouse, parent, or guardian of the victim[32] It includes a "withheld conviction" under federal law.

These disabilities are imposed by federal law, and violations are taken very seriously by your friendly federal government, and BATF agent (Bureau of Alcohol, Tobacco, and Firearms). They apply equally to sales by licensed dealers, and private individuals. Florida has similar laws in F.S. 790.065(2)(c)(1); and F.S. 790.233. Moroever, Florida defines "domestic violence" somewhat different than federal law.[33]

PURCHASE FROM A LICENSED FIREARMS DEALER:

In order to sell firearms, as a business, a person or corporation must be federally licensed. This requirement does not apply to the sale of ammunition[34], although a federal licensee who also sells ammunition must comply with certain federal laws that a non-licensee who sells ammunition, does not. Whatever, anybody who sells firearms as a part of his business with the idea of making a profit vs. enhancing his personal collection -- must be licensed by the feds. A failure is a very unpleasant federal prison sentence. This requirement applies to pawnshops, antique dealers, or whoever. Only sales from legitimate private collections are exempt -- and these better be very on the level.

Now, purchasing a firearm from a dealer is a very different animal than buying it privately. There are alot more regulations that you both have to comply with, certain forms, record checks, and you may find that while you could legally buy the same gun from a private person -- you can't legally purchase it from a dealer. Doesn't make much sense, does it?

QUESTION: What are the differences in a private sale?

ANSWER: No 3 day waiting period on a handgun. No FDLE background check, or federal form to fill out, no requirement that handgun purchaser be 21 years old. Eighteen years old would be sufficient. Same age of eighteen applies to rifles and shotguns. But you still can't sell to someone from out-of-state, a convicted felon, etc.

I guess you'd really like me to get into the meat and potatoes of this section, so let me get on with it, and fill you in on the regulations, and procedures for an over-the-counter purchase that I haven't already specified.

FLORIDA FIREARMS PURCHASE PROGRAM:

Florida has instituted, amongst other things, a firearms purchase program administered by the Florida Department of Law Enforcement (FDLE). This program requires any firearms dealer to run a criminal history records check of any prospective purchaser over the phone on a special line to FDLE. There is an eight dollar service fee which is charged to the potential purchaser, even if the sale cannot be completed.

The records check is a mandatory requirement to purchase a firearm from a licensed dealer, unless the potential purchaser has a valid Florida Concealed Weapons Permit issued prior to 11/30/98 , or holds an active Florida certification as a correctional or law enforcement officer. If the purchaser has such a certification, or the Concealed Weapons Permit, no check is necessary, although you still must fill out the Form 4473.

The records check searches the person's record for anything that would prevent them from purchasing or possessing a firearm under both federal and Florida law. If anything is found, the purchase will be disapproved. However, it could miss an old battery or assault conviction or "withheld adjudication" that now qualifies as a "domestic violence" crime.

ARREST FOR "DANGEROUS" CRIME, PENDING DISPOSITION:

If you are trying to purchase a firearm from a dealer, and have been "arrested" (no trial, or plea -- just the arrest) for what is considered a "dangerous crime" under F.S. 907.041(4)[35], or for certain other specified felonies, under Florida law you will not be able to purchase the firearm, unless the case was dropped, and there is proof of this. This is also true if you have been formally charged with any of these crimes, have a domestic violence or repeat violence injunction entered against you, have a conviction for domestic violence, or are formally charged with the commission of any felony, because an Information or Indictment has been filed against you in a court of law.

The list of arrests that bar your approval from purchasing from a firearms dealer, including any attempt or conspiracy to commit them, are found in the following table:

CHART OF ARRESTS PREVENTING FDLE APPROVAL:

arson *	aggravated assault *	aggravated battery *	sabotage
child abuse *	hijacking *	kidnapping *	homicide *
illegal use of explosive*, & other explosives violations	robbery*	sexual battery *	indecent or lewd assault or act on or in presence of child under 16 *
		any child abuse*	
sexual activity with child 12 - 17 by or through person in custodial or familial authority *	burglary of dwelling *	criminal anarchy (felony only)	extortion
	carjacking*	domestic violence	abuse of elder or disabled*
	hijacking *		
explosives violations *	any C.893 controlled substance violation	resisting officer with violence	any C. 790 weapon or firearms charge
treason	assisting suicide	manslaughter *	any stalking *

* includes attempt or conspiracy to commit

SOME OTHER DISABILITIES:

Section 922 (b)(2) of the federal Gun Control Act of 1968 states that it is illegal for a licensed dealer to transfer a firearm to any person whose purchase or possession would be in violation of State law. Florida law does not seem to permit the following additional persons to possess firearms, so I assume they would also be legally excluded from purchasing from a licensed dealer, although this may constitute a loophole for sale from a private individual. Even if this loophole exists, it would be risky, and could subject you to some very costly civil liability if something went amiss. Anyway, here's the additional list:

a.   Person who is a habitual or chronic alcoholic.
b.   Vagrants
c.   Person on Florida probation

PERSON ON FLORIDA PROBATION:

Ah, yes! The zinger of Florida law! A person on any type of Florida probation cannot possess, carry, or even **own** a firearm — unless authorized by the court, and consented to by the probation officer.[36]

QUESTION: You mean that if I get a lousy DUI, I've got to sell my firearms?

ANSWER: Yes — amazing, huh? It applies equally to misdemeanors, felonies, and even criminal traffic offenses where probation is imposed — at least, unless you can get the judge and probation officer to agree otherwise.

QUESTION: How could I own or possess a firearm on felony probation, even with the agreement of the judge and probation officer? Isn't that always illegal?[37]

ANSWER: If you had a "withheld adjudication" you would not be a "convicted felon", and could technically still own firearms if you could get this permission. I assume it would have to be by a written order of the judge to be valid. Same theory applies on a misdemeanor (adjudicated or withheld) except domestic violence.

QUESTION: So, what happens once I'm off probation?

ANSWER: Unless you were convicted of a felony, the "proba-tion" restriction disappears.

EFFECT OF A FELONY RECORD ON THE FDLE CRIMINAL HISTORY SEARCH:

The criminal history check run by FDLE will also search to see if you have any felony "convictions", or if you received a suspended sentence, or a "withheld adjudication" for any felony. If you were actually "convicted" of the felony -- you will not be eligible to purchase, own, or possess a firearm under any circumstances -- unless the legal disability has been removed. See a lawyer, or read the chapter on disability removal.

THREE YEAR WAITING PERIOD:

If you received a suspended sentence, or a "withheld adjudication" on a felony -- then you can't get an FDLE approval until you have ex-punged your record, or three (3) years has passed from the date that your probation was over, or any of the conditions set by the court have elapsed. Once the 3 years is up, you're eligible to purchase from a dealer again, however, the loophole here is pretty clear -- you can still purchase from a private individual.

One word of caution. Don't get a friend to buy you a firearm from a dealer, or anyone else if you don't qualify under these sections. This is called a "straw man" transaction, and is a state and federal crime. If you do, both you and your friend will be guilty of a felony.[38] Same thing goes for giving false identification.[39]

WAITING PERIOD FOR HANDGUN PURCHASES:

A few years ago Florida passed a constitutional amendment that provided a three (3) business day waiting period (weekends and legal holidays don't count) for the purchase of a handgun unless you have a concealed weapons permit.   In November 1998 another amendment changed this somewhat, and now each county may place a waiting period of up to five (5) days on any firearm — if any part of the transaction takes place on public property. This applies to most gun shows because they are often held in government owned convention centers. It also applies to streets, sidewalks, parks, etc.   It does not apply to a private home, business, property, or stores.   Each county may also require a criminal history records check on private sales conducted on public property. Again, this is a county-to-county thing. However, neither provision applies to sales to a concealed permit holder. It also should not apply to trades, where it's strictly gun-for-a-gun. Police officers are not exempted from these requirements unless they have a concealed permit.

If you think this is kind of stupid — you're right. They could have passed this in the legislature by statute. To do it by constitutional amendment was absurd. However, almost everybody in Florida voted for it. Score another one for ignorance, and the media. So, here's my quote for the day:

"Experience should teach us to be most on our guard to protect liberty when the Government's purposes are beneficial . . . . The greatest dangers to liberty lurk in insidious encroachment by men of zeal, well-meaning, but without understanding."   Justice Brandeis in Olmstead v. United States, 277 US 438 (1928).

QUESTION: So, if I have a concealed permit, I don't have to wait three days to get my handgun?

ANSWER: Right.   Florida now checks both concealed permit applications, and firearm purchases through the National Instant Check System computer system (NICS).

CHART OF PERMITTED/NON-PERMITTED SALES:

CHART OF PERMITTED/NON-PERMITTED SALES:

	HANDGUNS		RIFLES & SHOTGUNS	
	Private	Dealer sales	Private	Dealer sales
Age	18 years	21 years old	18 years	18 years old
Residence	same state	same state	same state	any state
3 Day Wait	none	yes, except CWP holder	none	none
Felony conviction	not allowed	not allowed	not allowed	not allowed
Felony "withheld"	allowed	after 3 years	allowed	after 3 years
"Dangerous crime" arrest	allowed	not allowed	allowed	not allowed
Indictment or Information for felony	not allowed	not allowed	not allowed	not allowed
fugitive	not allowed	not allowed	not allowed	not allowed
unlawful drug user	not allowed	not allowed	not allowed	not allowed
illegal alien	not allowed	not allowed	not allowed	not allowed
mental defective or was committed	not allowed	not allowed	not allowed	not allowed
dishonorable discharge	not allowed	not allowed	not allowed	not allowed
renounced citizenship	not allowed	not allowed	not allowed	not allowed
conviction of domestic violence, or restraining order	not allowed 18 USC 922(d)(8)	not allowed	not allowed	not allowed
legal aliens	not allowed	may be allowed	not allowed	may be allowed
Probation in Florida	not suggested	not allowed 18 USC 922(b)(2)	not suggested	not allowed
chronic or habitual alcoholic	(?) not suggested	not allowed	(?) not suggested	not allowed

CHAPTER THREE

WHAT TO DO
AFTER THEY TURN YOU DOWN

Ah, ha! They turned you down. Those lowly pencil-pushing, dirty so and so's had the nerve to turn you, the all-knowing, all-seeing, all-perfect one, down! A pox on all of them! What do they know?

Well, that's actually a good question, Oh Knowing One. You've raised an interesting point.

To answer that, let's first see how it actually works in FDLE Land. It may surprise you. And, by the way, these are generally pretty nice people . . . so don't get down too hard on them. If problems arise -- it's usually not their fault.

THE APPROVAL (OR DISAPPROVAL) PROCESS:

In 1989 Florida passed a law requiring licensed firearm dealers to do a telephone records check on non-licensee purchasers with the FDLE prior to completing any sale. The purpose of the law is to do a statewide and national criminal records check before an approval for purchase is given. Philosophically speaking, this is a pretty good idea. A rare thing in government. It was also pretty good anticipation of the Brady Bill. Score one brownie point for Florida!

Anyway, under Florida law, sales of firearms between private individuals from their private collections are normally not covered by these "record checking" regulations, although sales between private individuals are still subject to certain federal and state restrictions, and in certain counties, sales on public property may require a record check, and even a three day wait on certain purchases to non-permit holders. Otherwise, there currently is no FDLE check in a private sale. However, since we're now talking about dealer sales, and not staring into a crystal legislative ball -- let's get back to the subject at hand.

IDENTIFICATION NECESSARY:

The procedure is for the dealer to have the prospective buyer, including any individual wishing to trade an old firearm for another one, to complete a federal **Form 4473** -- the form that any purchaser must fill out, when purchasing a firearm from a licensed firearms dealer. The purchaser must also furnish photo, and other identification which establishes his or her name, residence address, race, sex, date of birth, and some type of identification number.[40] Photo identification is normally done by a drivers license, or state identification card. Other acceptable photo identification includes a Concealed Weapons Permit, Military identification card, passport, immigration card, or employment/school identification. Production of your Social Security card is also recommended, although not necessary, as it does provide another identifying number in the computer systems which could clear-up any potential misidentification when FDLE does the records check. An eight dollar processing fee is then collected, and the dealer calls FDLE at a special toll-free number.

THE COMPUTER CHECK BY FDLE:

At this point the FDLE operator conducts a computerized state and national criminal records check. Based on the findings of that check the operator will provide the dealer with an approval, non-approval, conditional approval, or conditional non-approval number. The operator is <u>not</u> allowed to release any criminal history over the phone, and the dealer may not ordinarily reveal the results of the check with anyone except the buyer.[41] Of course, giving false information to the firearms dealer in order to secure a firearm is also a state and federal crime -- a felony.[42]

HOW THE FDLE CALL-IN SYSTEM OPERATES:

When FDLE gets the call, they have a limited amount of time to make a determination of your eligibility, assuming your record is unclear. The <u>maximum</u> delay is 24 working hours. "Working hours" mean

Monday to Friday, from 9:00 a.m. to 5:00 p.m., legal holidays excluded. If the record shows no disability -- the approval is immediate.

If FDLE can't make a determination one way or the other within this time frame, the dealer is given a CONDITIONAL APPROVAL NUMBER, and you are allowed to purchase the firearm. However, if FDLE receives information at a later time that you were really ineligible, this conditional approval is revoked, the conditional approval number becomes a "non-approval number", and local law enforcement is alerted. Obviously, you can't keep the firearm, and that brings up some interesting civil questions on whether the dealer would be obligated to take it back, and give a refund.

If you have a pending arrest on any "dangerous crime", domestic violence, or one of the special enumerated felonies I listed in the last chapter -- you get a CONDITIONAL NON-APPROVAL until the case is disposed of, and you inform FDLE that you're now off-the-hook. At that point, if you check-out as OK -- the qualified non-approval number becomes an approval number. If an Indictment or Information is filed against you for any felony (not just an arrest), then the same rule applies, and you receive a conditional non-approval until the case is resolved in your favor. If resolved against you, your conditional non-approval becomes a literal non-approval.

Obviously, if the check comes back that you have a felony conviction, are a deserter, were found mentally incompetent, or had some other legal disability, you will be disapproved. Same thing if it comes back with a withheld adjudication on any felony unless three (3) years have elapsed from the date all probation and any other conditions set by the court, including restitution, have been completed. If the amount of probation is unknown, then FDLE will use the three years, as a rule of thumb, until it can be shown otherwise.

Whatever happens, the dealer writes the approval, non-approval, conditional approval, or conditional non-approval number on the upper right hand corner of the Form 4473. He retains this in his records, and you do not get a copy -- so don't bother trying. The records are confidential.

WHAT HAPPENS IF THE COMPUTERS ARE DOWN:

If computers are down -- FDLE has until end of next business day (5:00 pm) to notify the licensed firearms dealer that the purchase is prohibited. Otherwise, they must issue an approval, or conditional approval number, and you can purchase the gun.

The "next business day" is a Monday thru Friday, holidays excluded. This is true even though FDLE is required to have these phone lines working 7 days a week, 9:00 a.m. to 9:00 p.m. -- except Christmas and New Year's Day.

If telephone service is not working at the licensee's premises due to the fault of the telephone carrier, or because of any natural disaster, act of God, war, invasion, insurrection, riot, other bona fide emergency, or any reason truly beyond the control of the licensee, then the FDLE phone check and approval is not necessary. In that case, all that's done is fill-in, and sign the federal Form 4473, and if everything else is OK -- you can buy the gun, then and there.

PROBLEMS WITH MIS-IDENTIFICATION:

When you apply for the records check, the computer is trying to match you with millions of disqualified people. If somebody has the same name, sex, date of birth, and skin color -- you've got a problem. Same thing if somebody else has been using your name, or identification illegally. Since the law of averages says that this is very possible -- problems can occur. A non-approval usually happens like this:

a.   All identifying data in the inquiry matches.

b.   Where it's for a female, if there's a match on race, date of birth, social security number, and first name.

c.   Regarding possible misspelling matches -- where the first name of the applicant has another common spelling or ending (Bill, Billy, Billie, William, Wil, etc.); or the last name has a common similar spellings or ends in "s" or "z" (Rodrigues, Rodreques, Rodreguez, Rodriguez).

d.   Regarding, possible name matches --where the purchaser gives a full name, and there is a match with a person with the same last name who has a matching initial for the first or middle name.

APPROVAL, OR NON-APPROVAL NUMBERS FROM FDLE:

Once you're approved, the approval number is valid for a total of thirty (30) days from issuance, or until the purchase transaction is completed. It expires upon use. If a non-approval number is assigned, the sale cannot be completed, and the dealer is supposed to advise the purchaser of his right to "appeal" the non-approval. There is a form for doing this which the dealer is supposed to provide, and he also should complete the "dealer" section. Any appeal must be filed within 21 days.

If the "appeal" is successful, FDLE sends the buyer a letter notifying him that the firearm may be purchased. The buyer may bring the letter to any dealer who can then make a sale without any further FDLE check. The letter will have a cut-off date, after which it becomes invalid. The letter is then kept by the licensed firearms dealer, and attached to the federal Form 4473. This "appeal" procedure is explained in the next section.

APPEAL PROCEDURE & CRIMINAL HISTORY REVIEW:

Actually, this "appeal" procedure is not really an appeal, but is a formal "criminal history records check", where you provide FDLE with your fingerprints to assist a more in-depth examination of the (hopeful) mix-up. There is no charge for the records check by FDLE, but you must obtain a set of your fingerprints from a local law enforcement agency on the appropriate fingerprint card (FBI FD-258), or on the fingerprint portion of the appeal form. The local agency may charge you a fee for doing the fingerprinting, although the Sheriff is supposed to do it for free, upon request. Once you have the fingerprinting done, you send the card and the "Firearm Purchase Non-Approval Appeal Form" to FDLE, on the address listed on the form. Make sure the card is in an appropriate envelope, because a bent fingerprint card is not going to do you much good if somebody is trying to compare prints. The address is:

FDLE
Firearm Purchase Program
Post Office Box 1489
Tallahassee, Florida 32302-1489

If a positive fingerprint identification is made against an existing criminal record, then FDLE will return the fingerprint card, appeal form, and a single copy of the record directly to the applicant, unless you submitted it through a law enforcement agency. If you still think there is a mistake, there are additional procedures you may follow, but they get very complicated, and I suggest you hire an attorney to assist you with them. Again, FDLE must receive your "appeal" within 21 days of the denial — otherwise you're out of luck.

A QUICK HINT:

If you get turned down, and think it's a mistake -- you may be right. Sometimes the FDLE operator punches in the wrong information (hey, they're human!), and you get a disapproval. If this happens, don't despair. Try again a day or two later, and it will probably be approved. If not -- then, you may have a problem, and will have to get a criminal history records check through the appeal process I've already explained.

THE BRADY ACT & NICS:

The Brady Act's[43] permanent provisions went into effect on November 30, 1998. It did not substantially affect Florida, since many of its provisions were already operational here. There were some brief problems due to Federal law requiring background checks through the new NICS (National Instant Check System) system, as that computer system has a wider data-base than what Florida used to use to approve concealed permits. The NICS system check includes domestic violence injunctions, misdemeanor domestic violence, etc. Florida began using NICS for both the concealed permit, and firearm purchases in November 1998 — so no problem.

Other than that, Brady's provisions require multiple sales of handguns be reported by dealers on both the ATF form, as well as to State or local government -- so that your local police, etc., will now have a "track" of purchasers buying more than one handgun in a week's time from the same dealer. Aside from this, it raised the application fee for becoming a federally licensed dealer, and requires that proof of your pre-November 1998 concealed permit be attached to the Form 4473 by the dealer in order to avoid a NICS check. Where you qualify, this is accomplished by the dealer photocopying your permit and attaching it to the form. If you do not have a concealed permit, you must still wait three days to purchase a handgun. There is no waiting period on a rifle or shotgun as long as you got the FDLE approval or qualified approval which is being run through the NICS system.

A portion of the Brady bill was declared unconstitutional by the United States Supreme Court in June 1997 as being beyond the powers of Congress in the case of <u>Printz v. United States</u>.

CHAPTER FOUR

REMOVAL OF LEGAL DISABILITIES

Sometimes the computers are right -- and there's really no mistake about it. You've got a felony conviction, or other type of legitimate legal disability. Since the rest of us are now somewhat concerned that you may not be the type of person we really want walking around with a firearm -- you may be wondering what your options are. That's what this chapter is all about.

EXECUTIVE CLEMENCY:

The Florida Constitution, Article 4, section 8, grants the governor, with the approval of three (3) members of his cabinet, the ability to grant full or conditional pardons, and restore the civil rights of most individuals. This is also known as the right to "executive clemency". You have no individual right to executive clemency -- it is totally in the discretion of the governor and his cabinet. That means if you're denied -- tough luck! There's no appeal!

PARDON POWER:

There are certain statutes that cover the suspension of civil rights in Florida. These are found primarily in Florida Statute 944.292, which states that upon conviction of a felony, a person's civil rights "shall be suspended" until such rights are restored by a full pardon, conditional pardon, or restoration of civil rights. Although the legislature has passed laws concerning the suspension of civil rights, only the state constitution and governor have the power to decide how a person's civil rights will be restored. This procedure is set forth in the rules governing the Office of Executive Clemency.

Some of the exciting things that the governor can do would be to grant a full or partial pardon. A "full pardon" unconditionally releases you from any punishment left (although there usually isn't any), and forgives guilt. Any legal disabilities you had disappear, including the prohibition against possessing firearms.

A "conditional pardon" releases you from remaining punishment, and forgives guilt -- only if you meet certain conditions set in the pardon. If you fail to do them, you can be returned to your former status of legal slimeball. A conditional pardon does not authorize you to own, possess, or use firearms unless that right is specifically granted. You would still maintain this legal disability unless the conditional pardon restored your right to own and possess firearms.

Your application for pardon will be rejected unless you have completed all aspects of your sentence, and ten (10) years or more have passed since these were completed. If this sounds confusing, since I just told you that all aspects of the sentence had to be complete by at least ten years -- let me unconfuse you. Like everything else in life -- there are exceptions to the general rule, and there is a special procedure for waiver. I'll explain that later, as well as some other requirements of getting a pardon.

RESTORATION OF CIVIL RIGHTS:

It used to be that a restoration of civil rights was insufficient to remove legal disabilities to firearms ownership without also going through an additional approval with BATF in Washington, D.C. Due to a change in federal law this is no longer true, unless you had a federal conviction. To understand how it works, you need to know the following:

The federal definition of a "conviction" is set forth in 18 USC 921 (a)(20)(B), and states:

> "What constitutes a conviction of such crime shall be determined in accordance with the law of the jurisdiction in which the proceedings were held. Any conviction which has been expunged, or set aside or for which a person has been pardoned or has had civil rights restored shall not be considered a conviction for purposes of this chapter, unless such pardon, expungement, or restoration of civil rights expressly provides that the person may not ship, transport, possess, or receive firearms."

Do not read this section literally. The restoration must be total. Florida has something called a "Restoration of Residence Rights in Florida" which restores all civil rights except the right to own, possess, or use firearms. If you want a full restoration of civil rights -- it must also include the "Specific Authority To Own, Possess, or Use Firearms." If it doesn't -- you're still illegal, and mere temporary possession of a firearm would be a very serious state and federal felony.

In order to apply for the full restoration, you must have completed all aspects of your sentence, including monetary requirements, and any parole or probation -- by at least eight (8) years, and have no outstanding criminal charges pending anywhere. You must also be a resident of the State at the time the application is made, considered, and decided.

If all you want is a partial restoration -- you can apply anytime you've finished all aspects of the sentence, and you must meet the same residency requirements. This may be a good idea to start with, as it should help get you the full restoration after the eight years is up. I highly suggest it if you're in this position.

APPLICATION FOR PARDON, OR RIGHTS RESTORATION:

If you think you qualify for either getting a pardon, or restoration of civil rights, the procedure is to obtain an application form by requesting it from:

Coordinator
Office of Executive Clemency
2737 Centerview Drive
Knight Building, Suite 308
Tallahassee, Florida 32399-0950

Once requested, the application will be sent to you together with a short instruction booklet. In addition to filling out the form, you will need to attach to it a certified copy of any document that charged you with a felony of which you were convicted (ie: the Indictment or Information), as well as a certified copy of the judgement and sentence -- this goes for every felony you were ever convicted of, even if they are from out of state, or are federal convictions. While this may cause you quite a bit of legwork -- dems de rules!

While you are allowed to complete and handle this whole procedure yourself, you're probably better off with an attorney --

assuming he knows what the heck he's doing. You may want to think about this if it's important to you.

If your application is turned down -- do not totally despair. You may reapply any time after a year after the denial has gone by.

OUT OF STATE, AND FEDERAL CONVICTIONS:

The governor of the State of Florida has the power to grant clemency only on convictions obtained in a Florida State court, as far as possessing firearms go. Therefore, you must obtain separate restorations for federal and out-of-state convictions in order to legally possess a firearm. If somebody tells you otherwise, don't believe him. The law went through a radical change in 1994 when the United States Supreme Court, in <u>Beecham v. United States</u>, 511 U.S. 368 (May 1994), reinterpreted the federal statute that governed this. The change was not for the better.

AUTOMATIC GRANT OF PARTIAL RESTORATION OF CIVIL RIGHTS:

While this procedure won't get you your firearms rights back, it does get the ball rolling. Therefore, I strongly suggest pursuing it. If you qualify for this procedure, you can get an automatic <u>partial</u> restoration of your civil rights once you have properly filed and completed your application. Here are the requirements:

    a.   All aspects of sentence are totally complete, no other waiting period is involved.

    b.   No detainers or pending criminal charges of any kind.

    c.   No fines, restitution, or court costs of any kind left to be paid, including any outstanding traffic fines.

    d.   Must be a Florida resident.

    e.   Must supply certified copies of all Indictments and Informations convicted of, including judgements and sentences.

f.   The applicant has no convictions of a capital crime or a life felony.

g.   The applicant has not had a previous restoration of civil rights.

WAIVER OF RULES:

Ah, yes. Some people have all the luck! On the other hand, they may be truly deserving, and in need of a special break. That's what the waiver process is supposed to take care of.   It is basically a two step process that requires filling out a special form called a "Request for Waiver", which is then considered by the Florida Parole Commission. The Parole Commission then makes a recommendation on the waiver to the Clemency Board. If the Clemency Board approves it -- you still have to go through the application for executive clemency process. If not -- your application for clemency is stopped right there, without being considered. As with everything, you may retry after a year.

CASES OF EXCEPTIONAL MERIT:

If you have friends in high places, or have done something rather extraordinary -- you may have the proverbial "in". However, don't count on it. The governor, or any member of his cabinet may propose a person for executive clemency. If the governor, and three members of his cabinet approve -- it's granted just like that. No muss! No fuss! Nice to have connections, isn't it?

FLORIDA INTERPRETATION ON RESTORATION:

I need to mention one small additional problem if your conviction was from out of state, and you had your rights restored in the jurisdiction of conviction. In order to obtain a concealed permit here, the Secretary of State mistakenly thinks that the Governor of Florida still needs to grant you a restoration of firearms rights. This interpretation is patently wrong, and the courts have already decided that. But I'm not the one in control, here. The interpretation stems from a misinterpretation due to a change in federal law in 1994, and Fla. Admin. Code 27-5.009 (4) (e) of the

Rules of Executive Clemency which says a restoration restores to the applicant:

> "All or some of the rights of citizenship enjoyed before conviction in the State of Florida, or restores all or some civil rights in this State for persons convicted under the laws of another state or government."

What this section was supposed to do was allow somebody who moved into Florida to apply for restoration without having to go out of state, again. It was not to force somebody to go through the process twice. The case of <u>Schlenther v. Dept. of State</u>, 23 FLW 1562 (2DCA 1998) confirmed my view.[44] However, the executive department did nothing to change their regulations, and it still seems they may fight you on it, even though the case law is otherwise. The one exception they accept is where the conviction is expunged or vacated by the other state. In such cases, the Secretary of State interprets this as voiding the entire conviction as if it never occurred --.such that no restoration is needed.

FEDERAL PROCEDURE TO REMOVE DISABILITY:

18 USC 925 provides a federal procedure for the relief of legal disabilities. The other method is by presidential pardon. Other than a rather difficult court battle, these are the only two methods that exist for restoration of civil rights from a federal conviction. Unfortunately, Congress stopped funding ATF's overseeing the statutory procedure in 1992, and although it still exists on the books as a law -- it's no longer available as a practical matter. Start those presidential contributions rolling!

If you're curious to see how it should work, anyway, it starts by making application with Director of the Bureau of Alcohol, Tobacco, and Firearms (ATF). Any such application must include all the necessary court papers, including certified copies of the charging documents, judgement and sentence, as well as written consent to examine and obtain copies of your personal records, including background, medical, employment, military and criminal record. If you have received a pardon, expunction, setting aside, or other record purporting to show the conviction was rendered nugatory, or that your civil rights were restored, that should be included, too. However, you probably don't need the federal relief if they were, and it was a state court conviction.

If you were adjudicated a mental defective or were committed to a mental institution, a copy of the paperwork for the commitment proceeding is necessary, as well as any order showing discharge from commitment, and your restoration of mental competency, and other rights. Since you live in Florida, you would also have to comply with Florida law on this area.

If you were dishonorably discharged, you must provide a summary of service record, charge sheet, and final court martial order, and if you are an applicant who has renounced citizenship, you must include a copy of the formal renunciation made before a diplomatic officer, or equivalent.

Once you have provided all this pursuant to the application form required, the ATF Director may grant relief if it is established that the circumstances regarding the disability and applicants record and reputation are such that the applicant will not be likely to act in a manner dangerous to public safety, and that the granting of relief would not be contrary to the public interest. Moreover, the Director will not ordinarily consider granting relief until two (2) years have elapsed after your discharge from all terms of parole or probation.

However, as I previously stated, ATF is not doing removal of disabilities at this time. From a practical standpoint, that may mean that your only hope would be spending some serious money with a lawyer in a test case to try to get around this problem. There is some authority that this is possible if you can show a "miscarriage of justice", and exhaustion of administrative remedies [45] Still, this would cost some bucks, and doesn't have a great success rate. Federal courts are rarely sympathetic to anyone but the federal government.

Well, that's it for this chapter, and I guarantee that you probably know more about executive clemency than almost anyone else in the state who's not directly involved in the process, or hasn't read this book.

CHAPTER FIVE

FLORIDA CONCEALED WEAPONS PERMIT

The best thing that ever happened to the honest Florida firearms, or weapons owner in the State of Florida is the Concealed Weapons Permit law. I say this because prior to the passage of this State law, every single Florida county had its own individual set of standards and regulations -- which drove everyone who was trying to be honest -- totally nuts, and left your ability to legally carry a firearm at the mercy of each particular Board of County Commissioners. Politics at its very worst! Of course, the criminals could care less, one way or the other -- but that's another story.

Today, if you meet certain specified qualifications -- you can legally carry a concealed firearm, or any other weapon, almost anywhere in Florida -- with certain exceptions which I will outline later in this chapter. Although the specific purpose of this legislation was to authorize the carrying of a firearm " <u>as a means of lawful self-defense</u>", you should remember that it's still only a license to "carry" the firearm (or weapon) in a concealed manner -- and does NOT necessarily include the use or display of such. The "use" aspect of having a firearm, or any other weapon, is still governed by the criminal laws, and the law of justification and self-defense. "Display" is covered by a number of criminal laws.

If you own a firearm, or any other weapon, I strongly recommend you obtain the permit. You will see why by the end of this chapter.

QUALIFICATIONS FOR THE CONCEALED WEAPONS PERMIT:

Obtaining a Florida Concealed Weapons Permit is a fairly reasonable procedure. It takes about three (3) months to get it, from the time you send in the application -- and lasts for five years before it must be renewed.

The basic qualifications for obtaining the Concealed Weapons Permit are as follows:

1.   You must be 21 years of age, or older.

2.   You don't suffer from any physical infirmity which prevents the safe handling of a weapon or firearms.

3.   You're not a convicted felon, unless your right to own and possess a firearm was restored by executive clemency.

4.   You have not been committed for drug abuse within three (3) years of the date of your application for the permit, nor have you been found guilty of any drug crime, including misdemeanor possession, within the same time frame. In this sense, "guilty" is the equivalent of either a conviction, or a withheld adjudication.

5.   You are not a chronic and habitual user of alcohol to the extent that your normal faculties are impaired. This situation is presumed to be true if you were committed for alcohol treatment pursuant to Chapter 396 of the Florida Statutes; were convicted of using a firearm while under the influence of alcohol or a controlled substance; were convicted of DUI two or more times within 3 years of your application; or have been deemed a habitual offender of the disorderly intoxication laws within 3 years of your application.

6.   You have not been adjudicated an incapacitated person under Florida Statute 744.331, or have waited five (5) years after such incapacity was removed by court order.

7.   You have not been committed to a mental institution, unless you have a certificate from a psychiatrist licensed in Florida that you have not suffered from any such disability for five (5) years.

8.   You have not had a withheld adjudication or suspended sentence on any felony, or misdemeanor crime of domestic violence unless three (3) years have passed since you

completed all probation, and any other conditions set by the court; or unless your record was expunged regarding the felony. A sealing would not be sufficient. Furthermore, be warned — Federal law does not permit firearms possession where you have a misdemeanor domestic violence conviction — "withheld" or not. This also applies to police officers, even on duty. F.O.P. v. United States, 173 F.3d 898 (DCC 1999)

9.   You were not found guilty of one or more misdemeanor crimes of violence, unless three (3) years have elapsed since you completed any conditions set by the court in your sentence, including probation, unless the record was sealed or expunged.

10. You have not been arrested or formally charged with a crime which would disqualify you from holding a permit if convicted, and the Department of State was not notified of such arrest or formal charge by a law enforcement agency, the court, or FDLE.

11. You are a resident of the United States, or are a consular security official of a friendly foreign government. (Yes -- you can be an occasional visitor to Florida, and still have a permit. But remember, it only applies in Florida, unless your home state has a reciprocal law).

There are also training requirements "to demonstrate competence with a firearm". These are to assure the State that you have some intelligent idea of what you can legally do with a firearm, and know how to use it. As varied as this qualification may be in application, it seems to be working extremely well. Very few concealed permit holders are getting in trouble with the law since the program started. The training qualifications can be any one of the following:

1.   Completion of any hunter education or safety course approved by the Game & Fresh Water Fish Commission, or similar agency of another state.

2.   Completion of any NRA firearms safety or training course.

3.   Completion of any firearms safety or training course, or class, available to the general public which is staffed by instructors certified by the NRA, Department of State, or Criminal Justice Standards & Training Commission, and offered by: (a) law enforcement; (b) a college or junior college; (c) a private or public institution, or organization; or (d) a firearms training school.

4.   Completion of any law enforcement firearms training or safety course, or class, offered for security guards, investigators, special deputies, or any subdivision of law enforcement or security enforcement.

5.   Presents evidence of equivalent experience with a firearm through military service (copy of Honorable Discharge, or DD214), or through participation in organized shooting competition.

6.   Is licensed, or was licensed to carry a firearm in this state, any county of this state, or any such municipality, unless the license was revoked for cause.

7.   Completion of any firearms training or safety course, or class, conducted by a state certified firearms instructor, or an NRA certified firearms instructor.

If your training is under subsection 2, 3, or 7 of the above — and you took your instruction on or after July 1, 1998 — the instructor must also certify you safely handled and discharged the firearm, as part of the course. This is technically a "one shot" requirement. F.S. 790.06(2)(h).

Once you complete the course, you enclose a photocopy of your completion certificate with the rest of your application form, and you send it to Tallahassee. If you don't have a completion certificate you may substitute an affidavit from the instructor, school, club, group, or organization that conducted or taught the course/or class that attests to your completion -- or participation in firearms competition.

COMPLETING THE APPLICATION PROCESS:

If you are applying for the permit for the first time the fee, at last glance, was a total of $117.00. This represents both the cost of the permit ($75.00), and the balance ($42.00)for processing the fingerprint card. If you are only seeking a renewal, the fee is $65.00, and further fingerprinting is not required. The fingerprint card for the initial application must be filled out in **BLACK** ink. If you use blue ink, or some other color to fill in anything on the fingerprint card -- it becomes trash, and you'll need another one. The fingerprint card, and almost everything else are supplied to you, on request, in a packet from the Florida Department of State. The address is:

> Florida Department of State
> Division of Licensing — Concealed Weapon Permits
> P.O. Box 6687
> Tallahassee, Florida 32314-6687

Fingerprinting can be done at any law enforcement agency, but the Sheriff is supposed to do it for no more than five dollars. You will also have to supply a color photograph taken within 30 days of your application which meets a certain required size format. Separate instructions on this come with your application packet, and most passport photos are OK.

If you are a law enforcement, corrections, or correctional probation officer, or hold active certification from the Criminal Justice Standards & Training Commission as such, you do not need a background check for the permit, nor do you pay a fee for such. However, you are still stuck with the application or renewal fee. Furthermore, if you are applying for the permit for the first time and held any such position -- and you retired within the year immediately preceding the date of your application -- all fees are waived, and it's a one-time freebie. As stated, this does not apply to renewals, but only to initial applications. If you are a judge, you still must establish proof of the training requirements - but that's it.[46]

PROHIBITED PLACES WITH CONCEALED PERMIT:

The issuance of a Concealed Weapons Permit allows you to carry any type of legal weapon in a concealed manner. Open (unconcealed) carrying of weapons and firearms are not covered by this law, and is explained in another chapter of this book. The permit covers all manner of concealed weapons -- from firearms, to knives, to stun guns, to mace, etc. The only exception is that it does not apply to an automatic, or select fire weapon (ie: "machinegun").[47] However, just because you have the permit does not mean that you can carry a concealed weapon anywhere you want. There are limitations. Some of these make good sense, some do not. Here's the full list of where you can't carry the weapon or firearm under your license:[48]

1.   Any police station or facility (Sheriff, FHP, local police, etc.)

2.   Any jail, prison, or detention facility.

3.   Any courthouse or courtroom, unless you're a judge. Also, a judge may issue an order allowing a person to carry a firearm in his courtroom.

4.   Any government meeting involving the governing body of a school board, county commission, city commission, or special district.

5.   Any meeting of the Legislature, or any of its committees.

6.   Any polling place.

7.   At any elementary school, secondary school, college, or university facility. The definition of a "facility" normally relates to buildings, and structures -- thus, an entrance road or parking lot should not ordinarily fall within this definition. However, there are no Florida decisions regarding this, and the interpretation, for now, is purely mine.[49]

      Under this subsection of the statute, F.S. 790.06(12), you are also prohibited from bringing your concealed weapon to any "area vocational-technical center", and any school administration building. A willful violation of any part of this subsection by a permit holder is a second degree misdemeanor.

There is an exception to the prohibition, as applied to colleges and universities only, and only where the permit holder is <u>also</u> a registered student, faculty member, or employee, and the weapon is a stun gun or other non-lethal electric weapon that does not fire a dart or projectile, and is designed solely for defensive purposes. Chemical weapons are <u>not</u> permitted. These persons may carry such a non-lethal electric weapon into buildings and structures on the college and university campus so long as it is concealed.

Why the legislature did not permit pepper spray and other similar chemical weapons is beyond me. Chemical weapons would seem to make more sense to carry than a stun gun — since a stun gun requires very close contact before it can be used. However, that's what the legislature has decided.

Whatever, you should also know that <u>F.S.</u> 790.115 confuses this particular subsection because it prohibits the possession of any firearm or weapon on the "property" of a school, school bus or school bus stop, and further prohibits the "<u>display</u>" of a weapon on such areas, as well as within 1000 feet of a school, if the display is done in the presence of others, and in a rude, careless, angry, or threatening manner — and not in lawful self-defense. However, it then exempts concealed permit holders from the penalties of <u>F.S.</u> 790.115, and refers to their punishment as a second degree misdemeanor under the concealed weapons statute, <u>F.S.</u> 790.06(12). From a logical standpoint, the only way to harmonize these two statutes together is to construe them to mean that if you are a permit holder, and are prohibited under <u>F.S.</u> 790.06(12), you've committed a second degree misdemeanor. A less logical interpretation would be that you must comply with F.S. 790.115, just like anyone else — but if you willfully disobey — the worst you get is a second degree misdemeanor. The courts have yet to resolve this, and the safer practice, no matter what the law is, is obvious.

Of course, if you follow my first interpretation of this

statute -- you'd better keep your weapon concealed, because you're definitely asking for trouble if you display it. Test case time.

8.   Any athletic event of a school, or college -- and also for any professional athletic event (Marlins, Dolphins, the Heat, Buccaneers, etc.) of all types. There is an exception to this prohibition only if the event is one that is related to firearms.

9.   Inside the passenger portion of any airline terminal, and the "sterile area" of any airport (ie: the X-ray machine checkpoint, and beyond). Usually the area reserved for passengers making flight departures, or arrivals.

        However, there is an exception for anyone who is a passenger, is in the terminal (but not the sterile area), and is carrying a firearm for shipment as baggage on an airline when that firearm is already unloaded, and encased in a locked container. More on that in the next chapter.

10.   Any other place a firearm is prohibited by federal law, including any federal office or building.[50] This means, amongst other places -- a post office. It does not mean a bank. If you go to a bank, and take out lots of money -- you may need a firearm. If you go to an ATM (automatic teller), and it's after hours, statistics show you'd better have one!

11.   In any portion of a restaurant, bar, nightclub, or other establishment licensed to serve alcohol for consumption on the premises (not a liquor store which only sells the packaged stuff vs. serving it) in the portion of the premises that is primarily devoted to that purpose.

        In other words, if you go into a restaurant, you can't go in the bar -- but you can sit at a dinner table, go to other places within the establishment not within the bar, and even order drinks with your meal, or just order drinks.

12.   Last but not least, you can't carry in a house of

prostitution, crack house, or place of illegal gambling, as these constitute "public nuisances" under Florida Statute 823.05.

LICENSE VIOLATIONS:

There are certain problems that can arise when you have the Concealed Weapons Permit. In comparison to what could happen to someone without the permit -- these consequences are really mild. One thing you need to know is that if you are carrying a concealed weapon or firearm, you must also have your actual permit on your person.[51] A failure to do so is a noncriminal violation with a $25.00 fine. Big deal! Same thing goes if a police officer asks to see your permit and other identification while you're carrying -- and you don't have it, or refuse to show it (that would be really stupid). Of course, you may get arrested for a felony since the officer is probably not going to take your word that you "must of left it at home". But, you'll finally be able to beat that charge, since you do have the permit somewhere. Of course, this will occur long after you are hassled-to-death by the system, as it tries to sort-out your screw-up.

Another problem is if you violate any of the use restrictions I just outlined in the preceding numbered paragraphs, 1 -12. If you do, and that violation was done "willfully" (ie: deliberate violation of the law)[52] -- it's a second degree misdemeanor. Moreover, if you do it at an airport -- it's also a federal felony, unless you can establish the defense that you are a total idiot, and really forgot that you had the .357 Magnum in your pocketbook. You'd be surprised how many people do this every year!

LOST LICENSES, OR CHANGE OF ADDRESS:

You are also required to notify the Department of State of any change in your permanent address, or if your permit was lost, stolen, or destroyed -- all within a period of 30 days. A failure is a noncriminal violation, and another big twenty five dollar fine. If you move, the process is real simple. You can mail or fax a letter (fax to: 850-487-7950) stating your new address, and asking that your records be changed to show this. Make sure you include your concealed permit number. No charge, unless you want to receive a replacement license. If you do, it's fifteen bucks, plus you need to send a color passport photo.

If it was lost or stolen, your permit is automatically invalid until you pay the Department of State a fifteen dollar ($15.00) fee to reinstate it, a photo, and you receive back the replacement license. In order to get this, you also have to send them a notarized statement that the permit was lost, stolen, or destroyed -- along with the fee, and the passport photo. The address for all of this is:

> Florida Department of State
> Division of Licensing
> Concealed Weapons Permit Program
> P.O. Box 6687
> Tallahassee, Florida 32314-6687

QUESTION: Does that mean that if I lost my original, but have a copy -- I don't have the protections of a concealed permit?

ANSWER: Silly, huh? Yeah, that's the way the statute seems to read. From a constitutional standpoint there may be a way around it, but who would want to be in that position? Remember, test cases are only good for lawyers.

SUSPENSION OR REVOCATION OF YOUR PERMIT:

The State is not happy if you suddenly do something you shouldn't have, and still have your permit to carry. Most of the time this makes good sense -- however, if you use your gun for self-defense, and get arrested because your friendly local State Attorney or police department are too chicken to stand-up against possible adverse publicity from local (anti-gun) media -- it (pardon the expression) stinks. However, this is not where I am going to lecture you on my personal philosophy of life, and firearms, so let's get back to the law.

If you plea or are found guilty to a felony while you hold the permit, obviously, it's history. Same thing if you get a conviction or "withheld" of any drug crime, misdemeanor or felony, or anything that is a misdemeanor or felony crime of domestic violence. You'll get a suspension if there's an injunction in effect that prevents domestic violence, or repeat violence. As to other exciting reasons why your permit will be revoked or suspended, here's the rest of the list:

1. committed as an alcoholic, or deemed a disorderly intoxication habitual offender.

2. convicted of a second DUI within 3 years of any prior one.

3. adjudicated an incapacitated person.

4. committed to a mental institution.

5. develops or sustains a physical infirmity which prevents the safe handling of a weapon or firearm.

6. chronically and habitually uses alcoholic beverages to extent that normal faculties are impaired.[53]

7. May revoke if licensee is found guilty of one or more crimes of violence within the preceding three years.[54]

8. Shall suspend the license upon notification by FDLE, a court, or law enforcement agency of the arrest or formal charge of a drug crime, a felony, a second DUI within three years, pending final disposition of the charge.

CHART OF WHY LICENSE CAN BE REVOKED:

REASONS FOR LICENSE SUSPENSION/CANCELLATION	
felony conviction	unsafe physical infirmity
mental commitment	adjudicated "incapacitated"
crime of violence within 3 years (discretionary)	2d DUI within 3 years
drug crime within 3 years	chronic drug/alcohol user

| drug/alcohol commitment | Agency notified of disqualifying charge/arrest |
| domestic violence conviction or "withheld" | current domestic violence or repeat violence injunction in force |

HOW YOU CAN CARRY CONCEALED:

Carrying a concealed weapon or firearm under F.S. 790.01 means "on or about your person". On or about your person generally means within your reach. Thus, you may legally carry your firearm or weapon in a briefcase, bag, etc. -- as well as on your immediate person, so long as it's concealed. Logically, this means you could have it within reach, under a towel in your car.

Now, just because this is legal, don't think you can't get arrested. The problem is that many police officers have not been trained very well in this area, and have their own idea of what the law is. I personally handle at least half a dozen cases a year where the police arrest someone for something that is totally legal. Unfortunately -- they just didn't know the law. More unfortunately, some innocent slob got arrested for being legal. That's life in the big city. It happens.[55]

The only thing I can tell you is that once you finish reading this book, keep it in your vehicle. Then if a police officer pulls you over, and suddenly announces you're being arrested for something the law says you can do -- you can politely tell him that you're sure he knows the law, and you don't want to sound like a "wise guy" -- but you've got this book on firearms in the car that's being used by seven police academies, and over seventy law enforcement agencies -- and it says that it's O.K. Would he please "just take a look?"

With a little bit of the Irish luck, he'll realize he may be making a slight error, and with even more luck, he'll say something to the effect of: "I don't care what the book says, I know the law. But, I'm gonna give you a break. Don't do it again."

At this point, thank him. Then, shut your mouth, and be thankful you didn't have to go to jail to prove your point. Got the point?

WHY CONCEALED PERMITS ARE THE BEST:

I'm the greatest believer in concealed permits there is. Well . . . at least, I'm one of them. I think that it takes the edge off situations where you might otherwise get arrested, and normally puts you in a position where a police officer will give you the benefit of a doubt. It also fills in the gaps where you need to carry concealed, or unintentionally do carry concealed. In other words -- it's there.

Maybe you have mace, maybe a stun gun, maybe a Taser, maybe a not-so-common pocket knife. Whatever -- you're covered with the permit!

More importantly, you join the ranks of over 230,000 active permit holders. Dems alot of votes, partner! The more permit holders there are, the less likely it will be that politicians are going to try to take any of your rights away. And, if you don't think there are forces out there that would love to see you disarmed, and easy prey for everything and everybody -- you better start getting educated, because the battle is raging around you, every single day.

RECIPROCITY OF PERMITS:

Out of state residents who are at least 21 years old, and have a valid permit in a state that recognizes Florida's concealed permit may use their permit when in Florida. These other states, as of September 1999, are: Arkansas, Georgia, Indiana, Kentucky, Michigan, New Hampshire, and Tennessee. Vermont permits concealed carry, but they have no permits — so they are not within the law. Remember, just as you must obey the concealed carry laws of these other states when you're there, so must a visitor from one of these states conform their conduct to Florida concealed law when here. See, http://licgweb.dos.state.fl.us/news

WARNING ABOUT DOMESTIC VIOLENCE:

One thing to remember — federal law has screwed-up Florida laws on misdemeanor domestic violence. Federal law says a "withheld" is a "conviction" for this purpose — no matter what Florida law says. Federal law this applies to police and citizens, alike. Federal case law says that even if your "Florida withheld" was ten years ago before there was such a thing as "domestic violence" — you qualify if the act alleged fits the current federal definition.   So, if you follow Florida law — you commit a federal felony.   Obviously, somebody in the Legislature needs to read this book, and as you probably have figured out by now — so does everybody else who owns a gun.

SUMMARY AND CHART:

Anyway, the real story about concealed carry is in the next chart. The figures speak for themselves, because the concealed weapon program has been going on in Florida since 1978, and the only thing the figures show is that the program works! People who take the trouble to get the permit -- rarely get in trouble!

CHART — STATISTICS OF CONCEALED PERMITS:

FLORIDA CONCEALED WEAPONS PROGRAM	
Applications received (10/87 - 2/28/99)	568,512
Applications denied	2,069
Licenses revoked	Crime before licensed - 383
	Crime after licensed - 767
	Those involving firearm -113
Total licenses issued	558,549
Total number of valid licenses on 2/28/99	230,326

CHAPTER SIX

TRANSPORTATION AND CARRYING OF WEAPONS, AND FIREARMS

When I do a speaking engagement, the questions I am asked most frequently are those related to the transportation of firearms. In other words: "Where the heck can I keep it, and how?"

Leading the confusion chart are questions relating to transportation of a gun in your own car while you're in Florida. But what about private boats, private aircraft, public aircraft, in a taxi, while you're camping, going to the range, going to a gun show, or traveling state-to-state in your car, etc.?

If you're a Concealed Weapons Permit licensee -- you have a much easier problem to contend with. However, with the number of state and federal laws that govern this area, the legal carrying or transporting of firearms, as well as other weapons, is far from simple -- permit, or not. That's what I'll try to show you in this chapter. And although the law is not perfectly clear on all points, I'll make it as clear as anybody can.

THE LEGAL CARRYING OF FIREARMS -- LISTED:

Since Florida generally prohibits open carry of firearms[56], and concealed carry of almost everything[57], there is a statute, F.S. 790.25, that gives certain listed exceptions to this. The statute seems contradictory in parts, but the case interpretations of the statute clearly indicate that these sections allow both concealed carry without a permit (except in private conveyances), and open carry. However, I advise you to use some discretion. Many police officers don't know this area of law — others don't care. You don't need to be a test case.

Anyway, here's the statutory list of exceptions to the general rule:

1.   Members of the military or National Guard, while on duty.

2.   Persons carrying out training for emergency management duties pursuant to Chapter 252.

3.   Law enforcement officers of this state; or those of other states, or the federal government while carrying out official duties in Florida.

4.   Florida or federal officials authorized to carry concealed weapons.

5.   Guards or messengers of common carriers, express companies, mail carriers, armored car carriers, banks, and other financial institutions while actually employed in and about the transportation or delivery of any money, treasure, bullion, bonds, or other thing of value within this state.

6.   Regularly enrolled members of any organization or club organized for target, skeet, or trap shooting, while at such practice or event, or going to or from such.

7.   Regularly enrolled members of clubs organized for modern or antique firearms collecting, while such members are at, or going to or from any gun show or exhibit.

8.   A person legally firing weapons for testing or target practice, under safe conditions, and at a safe place, or while going to or from such place, including an indoor range.

9.   A person engaged in fishing, camping, or lawful hunting, or going to or from such an expedition.

10.   A person engaged in the business of manufacture, repair, or dealing in firearms -- and any employee of such person while engaged in the lawful course of such business.

11.   A person who carries a <u>pistol</u> unloaded, and in a secure wrapper, from the place of purchase to his home or business, or to a place of repair, or back therefrom.

12.   A person at his own home or place of business (but this does <u>not</u> pertain to common areas shared with other individuals in an apartment building or condominium, or a shared parking lot).

13.   A person on a <u>public</u> conveyance transporting a securely encased weapon, which is not in his manual possession.[58]

14.   A person in a <u>private</u> conveyance (vehicle, aircraft, or boat) where the weapon is "securely encased", or not readily accessible for immediate use. However, in this circumstance the law says it <u>CANNOT</u> be carried on your person.

15.   An investigator employed full-time by the Public Defender or Capital Collateral Representative, in the course of their official duties, who meet other requirements of statute.

Now, if this list seems perfectly clear to you -- you are about the only person in the State who truly understands it, and when I quote this section of the law I do it with serious reservations as to whether some court will one day decide that a totally different interpretation should apply. Moreover, while some of these areas are pretty clear-cut, others are confusing as heck, and need explicit explanation. You may also have noticed that in some of these paragraphs I mentioned weapons other than firearms. However, most weapons other than firearms, are not regulated by Florida law unless they are carried "concealed". With only slight exception, it is technically legal to carry most weapons other than firearms, in the open -- just about anywhere. I'll cover that later. But since you still need some further instruction in the areas I've just covered in the preceding numbered paragraphs -- the next portion of this book contains the explicit explanation sections -- to whatever extent that is really possible.

LEGAL CARRYING AND TRANSPORTATION:

AUTOMOBILES AND OTHER PRIVATE VEHICLES:

The most often asked question in the State of Florida related to firearms -- is how can they legally be transported in a private vehicle. By "vehicle" I mean a car, truck, motorcycle, or any other type of private conveyance you can think of that normally drives on the road. By the word "private", I mean any vehicle that is not driven by somebody for hire, but is privately owned and driven. By "conveyance" I mean a trailer, motor vehicle, ship, railway car, or aircraft.[59]   A bicycle is not a conveyance.[60]

A vehicle that is driven in a car-pool is private, even if you all chip in on the gas. A non-private vehicle would include a taxi-cab, or rented limo. Any other interpretation of what is or is not private can probably be figured out by common sense. And by the way, these definitions were my interpretations, not the legislature's -- because the legislature didn't bother to give us any definition -- and the courts haven't gotten around to interpreting these definitions, either.

So, now that you know what is probably private, and what is not -- you still need to know the definition of the next two phrases: "securely encased", and "not readily accessible for immediate use". Each of these phrases apply to very different legal ways of transporting a firearm in your private vehicle. Here's how it works.

SECURELY ENCASED:

"Securely encased"[61] means that the weapon or firearm is in some type of holster, bag, enclosure, box, or container that is secured with a clasp, lid, zipper, strap, snap, Velcro, or other device, so that in order to fire or use the weapon, the device must first be opened, removed, or undone.[62] It does not require a lock. The purpose behind this was to give a person a very brief opportunity to think about it, before actually using it. This includes a closed glove compartment or console; zippered, snapped, or Velcro-closed bag,[63] holster, or case which first must be unclasped in order to fire; any type of box or enclosure with a closed lid; or even a purse -- assuming you can't operate the firing mechanism through the fabric, and there is some physical act required to open the top of the purse and unhook/unclasp/unzip it. A briefcase or suitcase also falls into this category. A cardboard box with the lid closed also complies.[64]

QUESTION: Can the gun be loaded if I do this?

ANSWER: Absolutely. It won't do you any good, otherwise.

QUESTION: I heard it must be in a holster if I have it in the glove compartment, and the glove compartment must be locked?

ANSWER: Nope. All you need is to have the glove compartment closed.

QUESTION: What if it's in my console, loaded, and ready to go?

ANSWER: Totally legal as long as the lid is closed.[65] If the lid is ajar, you're in big trouble.[66]

QUESTION: OK, I hear what you're saying, but I really don't understand. How can a firearm be "securely encased" if all I have to do is flip open a lid?

ANSWER: Well, it seems clear that the statutory definition of "securely encased" doesn't really mean that the weapon is "encased securely". It just means that the method of carry meets the statutory definition. If it does, it's "legally" secure, even if it's not factually secure.[67]

QUESTION: I've heard that keeping a firearm in a car is a two step, or three step rule. What does that mean?

ANSWER: It means that the person who gave you that advice couldn't remember what the statute actually said, so they made up their own definition to substitute for it. Forget it. Just remember the statute.

QUESTION: If a police officer stops me, and the gun is legally in my handbag along with my drivers license -- what do I do when he asks me for my license?

ANSWER: Make darn sure you take your drivers license out before you exit the car, and leave your purse inside. You are only legal inside the vehicle, unless you have a Concealed Weapons Permit. If you carry it outside -- it's a felony -- "carrying a concealed firearm". If it's another weapon other than two ounce chemical spray, a stun gun, or common pocketknife, it's a misdemeanor -- "carrying a concealed weapon".

If you tell him you have a firearm in the purse before you exit, and he thereafter tells you to hand it to him outside the car, you would have a legal defense since he ordered you to do it. Obviously, in this situation, don't hand him the firearm, itself! That would be stupid! He'll be nervous, and he also has a gun. Instead, give him the entire purse, and leave it closed, unless he instructs you otherwise. Or, stand away from the car, and have him take the purse out on his own. You don't want to get shot over a stupid misunderstanding

QUESTION: I live in a condominium. Can I take it from my car to my condo?

ANSWER: Not usually. Although you have the right to have it either in your car, or in your condo -- you cannot carry it across "common" areas -- such as a parking lot, elevators, or hallways -- unless you have the Concealed Weapons Permit. This was a major goof by the legislature.

68

QUESTION: What if I'm coming back from a hunting or camping trip?

ANSWER: Then it's OK, because you qualify under a <u>different</u> exception, <u>F.S.</u> 790.25(3)(h). Like I said before, you should be legal carrying open or concealed under this exception -- assuming the court interpretations stay consistent.

QUESTION: What if I'm in the car, and I put it in a paper bag, but I twist the top of the bag really well?

ANSWER: Technically, you may have a problem since the bag is easy to rip, and you may be able to pull the trigger through it. It certainly isn't a lid, zipper, snap, or anything similar. I wouldn't want to try it. Same thing for a cloth "Crown Royal" bag, which I seem to get a case on at least once per year.

QUESTION: What if I have it in an unsnapped holster?

ANSWER: If the gun is in a concealed area of the car, it's the third degree felony of carrying a concealed firearm. If the gun is in the open -- it's a second degree misdemeanor of "open carrying of weapons."[68] If the unsnapped holster is in the glove compartment, closed purse or briefcase, or closed console -- you're OK.

QUESTION: Why?

ANSWER: Because you're still legal under another part of the same section of the statute (ie: in a glove compartment, or other closed container).

QUESTION: What if I have it on my person in a snapped shoulder holster, but the holster can be detached intact from the shoulder harness?

ANSWER: Remember what I said before? It can't be on your person unless you have a Concealed Weapons Permit! If it is -- you are not protected by the law, and have committed a crime, whether it's securely encased, or not.

QUESTION: Is there any special place the firearm or weapon must be kept, if I have it in a securely encased bag or holster?

ANSWER: Nope.   Anywhere you want except on your person. It can even be under the seat -- as long as it's securely encased in a container or box with a closed lid; or a zippered, snapped, or Velcro-closed pouch, holster, or gun case.[69] Easy, huh?

READILY ACCESSIBLE FOR IMMEDIATE USE:

There's another legal way to transport a firearm in a private conveyance (ie: "vehicle") if it's not securely encased called "not readily accessible for immediate use".[70]

"Not readily accessible for immediate use" may sound like "securely encased", and to some extent there may be an overlap, but it's a separate concept entirely. Not readily accessible for immediate use means that the firearm or weapon cannot be used without some type of difficulty that significantly hinders it's immediate use. Court cases establish that this should include a loaded firearm with a trigger lock; or an empty firearm without any ammunition in "close proximity".[71] If the ammo was in the trunk it would be fine. Same thing if the ammo were in a locked box. Otherwise you're getting risky, and asking for a test case.

Another example of "not readily accessible for immediate use" occurs with a fully loaded firearm that just can't be used inside the vehicle, as a practical matter. Thus, in the case of Boswink v. State,[72] the appellate court held that a loaded shotgun and rifle in the back of a small pick-up truck was not "readily accessible" because the cab was too small to use the weapons from the inside without difficulty, and the occupant would normally have to exit the truck in order to retrieve, and use them effectively. Thus, they were not subject to retrieval "as easily and quickly as if carried on the person." Again, I wouldn't suggest relying on this case, too much. If you're truck or long gun was a different size — you might wind-up as another test case.

An interesting point not raised by the case is whether it's illegal to have an unconcealed, but loaded shotgun, or rifle in a private conveyance, at all. This question arises because F.S. 790.25(5), states that:

> "Nothing herein contained prohibits the carrying of a legal firearm other than a handgun anywhere in a private conveyance when such firearm is being carried for a lawful use."

If "legal firearm" means any legally possessed long gun not being carried for the commission of a crime. It"s legal. If "legal firearm" means a firearm being used within any of the exceptions stated in the "LAWFUL USES" section of F.S. 790.25(3) -- it gives it another meaning.

My vote is for the first meaning, because it makes more sense in the statutory scheme, and from a common sense standpoint. Dept. of Hwy Safety Legal Bulletin 88-02, which reviewed the 1982 enactment of this section also confirms my definition. This makes even more sense when you remember that our border states, Alabama and Georgia generally require open carry of rifles and shotguns in vehicles. Since a lot of north Florida residents hunt in these border states, I can almost guarantee that the language was included for that reason.

On the other hand, I don't know anyone who has ever raised this question in court before. I doubt it would go over real well in some of the more populated counties, legal or not. Get rural -- it would probably be another story. So, use common sense rather than becoming my famous "test case". It isn't worth the arrest — no matter what the outcome.

THE WAY IT USED TO BE:

I thought I'd get off the track here for a moment, and give you a little historical insight from our not too distant past. I get a perverse kick out of how some liberal legislators, and other "anti-gunners" think that permitting a firearm in a car is a recent, and overly generous gift to the citizens of Florida. If you look back into Florida's history, not all that far -- you'll find it wasn't originally thought of as a gift -- but was thought to be pretty much a basic right -- part of the right of an individual to self preservation. So, just in case you'd like to see how it used to be viewed by the majority, let me give you a quote from the 1941 Florida Supreme

Court case of Watson v. Stone:[73]

> "The business men, tourists, commercial travelers, professional man on night calls, unprotected women and children in cars on the highways day and night, State and County officials, and all law-abiding citizens fully appreciate the sense of security afforded by the knowledge of the existence of a pistol in the pocket of an automobile in which they are traveling. It cannot be said that it is placed in the car or automobile for unlawful purposes, but on the other hand it was placed therein exclusively for defensive or protective purposes. These people, in the opinion of this writer, should not be branded criminals in their effort of self preservation and protection, but should be recognized and accorded the full rights of free and independent American citizens."

INTER-STATE TRANSPORTATION OF FIREARMS:

If you are traveling from state to state in a private vehicle, the transportation of firearms and other weapons is governed by state, or by federal law. In Florida -- you know how you can transport it. But what happens when you get to the Georgia border, or beyond?

Federal law says that if you are traveling state to state, you can legally carry a firearm if such carriage is for a lawful purpose, and it would be legal for you to possess and carry it in your final destination state.[74] However, to qualify for this -- the firearm must be unloaded, and neither the firearm or ammunition can be readily or directly accessible from the passenger compartment of the transporting vehicle -- which means it should be locked in the trunk, unloaded.

When the vehicle has no separate compartment from the drivers compartment, then the firearm or ammunition must be kept in a locked container that is neither the glove compartment or the console. This section usually applies to trucks.

If you follow federal law, you may legally transport your firearms state to state, even if some of the intervening states would not otherwise permit it. Of course, don't take the gun out of this protected area until you arrive at your destination, unless you know that such would be lawful in whatever other state you are traveling in.

Federal law also permits that if there's a more liberal way of transporting the firearm in the state you're traveling in -- you can do it that way while you're in that particular state -- without losing your federal state to state protection during the rest of your trip. There's a book called "Traveler's Guide to the Firearms Laws of the Fifty States" written by attorney J. Scott Kappas in Kentucky. You can order it by calling (606) 647-5100. It's fairly inexpensive, and is worth the money. Tell them we sent you. Maybe they'll give my book a plug, in return.

The NRA also publishes summaries of the laws of each state. Give them a call, and if you're a member they'll send it to you.

PRIVATE BOATS:

Private boats that qualify as a "conveyance" are just like motor vehicles,[75] and the same state and federal laws apply with slight variation. The variation is that once you're outside the three mile limit on the east coast, or the nine mile limit (three leagues) on the Gulf Coast, you're in international waters -- and you can do most anything you want short of piracy, shooting at other people, boats, protected marine life, or carrying automatic weapons. Of course, once you come back into the jurisdictional limit -- make sure you're "Florida legal".

If you are thinking of traveling to the Bahamas -- their government told us not to take any handguns! You are allowed to have shotguns and rifles on board, but handguns are supposedly a definite no-no! Friends who travel to the Bahamas say this isn't so -- so, I guess you're on your own on this one. Under any circumstance, you will have to declare your firearms with Customs when you come into port.

If you are within the territorial waters of any other nation, you must comply with that nations laws. What that may be is outside the scope of this book, however, I understand that our jails are pleasure palaces next to those of nations south of the border.

COMMERCIAL AIRCRAFT:

If you are going to an airport as a passenger on a commercial aircraft -- you may take an unloaded firearm with you if it is checked-in as baggage, with the carrier. You must have any handgun placed unloaded, in a locked container -- and must declare any <u>firearm</u> at the main check-in counter. When I say "locked" -- I mean it must actually have a key or combination lock on it. While federal law only requires the lock for a handgun, many carriers require it for any firearm. Call the airline ahead of time to find out exactly what their policy is, and make damn sure you are legal in your destination airport.

Furthermore, don't try to declare it at the gate, because once you enter the "<u>sterile area</u>" you've committed a federal crime. If you don't remember what the sterile areas is, it's the area from the X-ray machine or security checkpoint, on. It's the portion of the passenger terminal usually reserved for the arrival and departure of passengers on scheduled flights. This rule applies equally to persons holding a Concealed Weapons Permit. Small arms ammunition should be securely packed in a box specifically used for ammunition. Declare that, as well.

PRIVATE AIRCRAFT:

When it comes to a private aircraft not being used for commercial purposes, you may carry firearms and ammunition according to State law, so long as it's done with the permission of the pilot. Ammunition should be limited to amounts that do not exceed a reasonable amount for personal use. The F.A.A. strongly recommends that ammunition be boxed in suitable containers. You may not carry any mace, or other chemical sprays, even if legal in your state as these are considered "<u>hazardous materials</u>". Of course, if you land at an airport, you are still subject to the rule about not having any ammunition, firearms, or weapons in the passenger "sterile area", and not having any firearm in the passenger terminal unless it is unloaded, and in a secured container.

TRAINS, BUSES, AND OTHER PUBLIC TRANSPORTATION:

If you are traveling interstate -- federal law controls, and you should deliver the firearm unloaded, in a locked container to the carrier for transportation, after declaring it as such. Again, I suggest calling the carrier before so you know their regulations.

If you are traveling by public transportation within Florida -- F.S. 790.25(3)(L) says the firearm or weapon must be securely encased, and not in your manual possession.[76] Since "manual possession" normally means that the weapon is actually in your hand -- my best guess is that "securely encased" should be a bit more secure than the normal definition.

Obviously, if you were holding a holster, it's probably in your manual possession, although "securely encased". If it were in a zippered gun case, you would seemingly be fine if you read this section literally. On the other hand, I think that prudence would dictate that it would be better if it could not be openly identifiable as containing a firearm. Therefore, I would have it securely encased in something inside my luggage, or contained in a locked briefcase, rather than in my hand. If I wanted to be extra careful — it would be unloaded.

Naturally, there is no case law interpreting this section, and there are just too many stories of law enforcement officials going on buses, and pressuring people into random searches -- and then seizing their firearms, whether they're legal or not. I wouldn't want you to be the test case if you were pushing this interpretation to the limit, so my advise is that it's better to be safe -- than sorry. Or — just get a Concealed Permit.

CARRYING IN YOUR HOME OR BUSINESS:

Now that we've beaten-to-death the subject of how you can carry a firearm (and any other weapon) in any type of vehicle or other transportation -- the next most important area is your home, or business. The good news is that you can carry or possess a firearm, or any other legal weapon, anywhere in your home or business, concealed or in the open -- your choice. No Concealed Weapons Permit necessary! This area of the law is very well settled.

The problems arise with getting the firearm to, or fro. This is where the Legislature goofed-up real good -- and was probably due more to oversight than anything else. So, what are the problems?

Problem number one is when you live in a condominium or apartment. When this happens, you must park in a common parking lot,[77] go through common hallways, use common elevators, and have access to common facilities. By "common" -- I mean that almost everybody in the complex has a right to use it. Unfortunately, unless you have a Concealed Weapons Permit, or you're coming back from a hunting, fishing, or camping trip -- or one of the other interesting exceptions I mentioned before -- you can't legally carry while you're on or in any of these "common" areas, concealed or otherwise.

QUESTION: So how the heck am I supposed to get my firearm from my car to my apartment?

ANSWER: You're not! Go get a permit, or tell your state legislator that the law is stupid as written, and you want it changed. Heck, it certainly is.

QUESTION: What if it's my own home, a duplex, and I'm renting the other half?

ANSWER: No problem for you, and no problem for your renter as long as you don't share any common areas. Technically, since you're the sole owner, and the other guy is only a renter -- he can't use the common areas for carrying a firearm, but you can.

QUESTION: What if I hear a noise on the stairway outside my apartment, and I think it's a burglar?

ANSWER: Another interesting test case. Technically, you have no right to go out with a firearm on a common area. However, since you do have a constitutional, and statutory right to self-defense, and defense of property -- you may have an exception to the general rule. Get a good lawyer.

As you can see from these questions and answers -- there are certain restrictions on carrying if you don't live in a private residence. If you do live in a private residence, even if you rent it -- you have a right to carry and possess firearms anywhere on the property, not just inside the dwelling.[78] Same thing if you're renting a room in a motel, as far as the room itself goes. It's your "dwelling", although temporary.[79] Since your property includes the driveway -- no problem getting the gun from the car to the house. This applies to every member of your family.

However, what about your business? In fact, what about an employee at his workplace? Well, the law says you can carry it concealed or in the open at your "place of business."[80] Employees are included in this provision even if the boss doesn't allow it. Of course, you can get fired if you do.

I also assume that the safe way to interpret this section of the statute would be to keep shy of parking lots shared by numerous businesses, and other clearly common areas — just in case the courts decide to treat this exception like a condo owner.

> QUESTION: I'm a construction worker, and I'll be working on a project at one location for the next six months. Does that qualify as "business premises"?

> ANSWER: I seriously doubt it. However, the construction trailer of the company you work for should. Test case time.

> QUESTION: I heard that you couldn't shoot anyone except if you were in your house. So, how can I legally carry a gun outside my home, even if it's on my property?

> ANSWER: You are confusing two different areas of the law. You're thinking about the "retreat rule" or "castle doctrine" which will be extensively discussed in a later chapter on self-defense, and which is really concerned about the use of a firearm, rather than when and where you can carry it. In essence, that particular doctrine is about when you must retreat, and when you may stand your ground without retreating. "Carrying" a weapon or firearm, is an entirely separate matter. The law says you can carry a firearm, concealed or in the open, anywhere on your property. In the house, in your business, or on the premises, outside. It doesn't matter. On the other hand, how you use it, does!

WHEN YOU STILL CAN'T HAVE IT:

There are always exceptions to the exceptions of legal possession and carrying. One big exception is when you're about to commit, or are committing a crime. Another concerns people in national forests. Another concerns schools. They uniformly apply to all persons, whether you have a permit or not. There are still other instances which could penalize otherwise legal possession, but let's just cover the areas I've mentioned, for now:

SCHOOLS, COLLEGES, UNIVERSITIES:

Rather than go over the rules that pertain to schools, and colleges -- let me tell you that this is gone over extensively in the chapter about children -- Chapter Eight. It's a real important area, and I highly suggest that you read it. Whether you have kids, or not, you'll find that it applies to you in some way.

NATIONAL FORESTS:

Except during hunting season, you can't have a firearm in a national forest unless you first get a permit from the county in which the forest is located. If it's in more than one county -- you've got to get permits from all counties involved, even if you only stay within the confines of one county. In order to do so you need written permission from the ranger in charge. If it's hunting season -- you need a valid hunting license. However, there is an effort to ban hunting in national forests, which could preclude all firearms there. If you're going into a national forest, national park, or other such area -- call their office ahead of time to see what the regulations are. Each one is different.

STATE FORESTS AND PARKS:

In Florida, Article 4, section 9, of the Florida Constitution gives the Game and Fresh Water Fish Commission jurisdiction to exercise:

> "regulatory and executive powers of the State with respect to wild animal life, and fresh water aquatic life."

Pursuant to these powers, the Commission has enacted a rather extensive set of regulations governing the possession and use of weapons within the boundaries of State parks, forests, wildlife management areas, etc. The same rule of caution applies -- before you go into one of these areas, call them on the phone, and find out what their regulations are. They should be able to supply you a written publication on their area, its rules, and a map of its boundaries. These are published by the State, and are made available to all citizens, for the asking. There is also a free annual publication for Florida hunters that gives an overall view of hunting regulations throughout the State. It's available at many sporting goods stores, driver license bureau's, and directly through the Commission in Tallahassee.

As a general rule, you will not be able to take any firearm, and certain other weapons on such property unless its during hunting season, and you have a valid hunting license. Even then, there are numerous restrictions, which you need to know. For now, these regulations are beyond the scope of this book.

SENDING FIREARMS THROUGH THE MAIL:

As a general rule, it is illegal to send any handgun through the mail. You can send a rifle or shotgun if you declare it as such -- but not a handgun. Send the handgun by a carrier such as UPS, but you must declare any firearm to the carrier in writing, and it must be unloaded and securely encased. You may only send a firearm out of state if it's for repair or return to a federal licensee, otherwise it is a federal crime, unless you are a federal firearms licensee.

QUESTION: What if I need to get a firearm repaired, and the factory is out of state?

ANSWER: You can mail it if it's a long gun, or UPS it if it's a handgun. However, the preferred method is never to send a firearm by the mail. By the way, Federal Express, or any other common carrier or trucker, can qualify for your shipment. I just know that UPS does alot of these. However, remember to declare it. Also, don't mark the package showing that the contents are a firearm. That's a no no, even if it's otherwise obvious.

QUESTION: What about mailing a hand gun to a relative within Florida?

ANSWER: Buy a toothbrush, and meet your new cellmate, Guido. However, you may legally UPS it (not the U.S. Mail) so long as it's within the same state you sent it from, and the person receiving it is not legally disqualified.

QUESTION: So, how the heck does my firearms dealer get his stuff, with all these regulations?

ANSWER: Try to remember that he's a federal licensee, and can receive or ship to or from any other federal licensee. The rules are different because of his qualifications.

CHAPTER SEVEN

COMMON WEAPONS VIOLATIONS AND RELATED CRIMES

The only people who don't have to worry about weapons violations are criminals, and juveniles who are becoming criminals. They don't care -- so whatever regulatory laws we pass aren't going to stop them. The only thing that will stop them is a jail sentence, and except for juveniles, we already have more than enough laws to accomplish that, if anybody would bother to enforce them. The rest of us who are just trying to defend ourselves, and stay out of trouble -- have all the problems obeying this stuff. Since you are hopefully in this later category of the population, God bless you, you need all the help you can get.

CARRYING CONCEALED WEAPONS AND FIREARMS:

By this time you should all know, with certain exceptions, that you can't carry a concealed weapon or firearm without a permit unless you're at home, or within your business premises. If you don't understand that by now -- you need a remedial reading course.

Carrying a concealed firearm without a Concealed Weapons Permit is a third degree felony. Carrying a concealed weapon, which is not a firearm, is a first degree misdemeanor, unless you have a permit. Of course, there are the exceptions that we've already discussed in a previous chapter, and a few more I'm going to update you on in a moment.

If you're an off-duty law enforcement or corrections officer, you can carry a concealed weapon or firearm only if you have a Concealed Weapons Permit, or if you have the permission of your superior to do so while off duty, for professional purposes. If your department has a written policy that you're always "on duty", even when not in uniform -- you're legal.[81] Otherwise, you're just like the rest of us.

81

Sometimes, people forget they are carrying a concealed weapon. This normally happens when they're in a rush, are preoccupied, and are legally transporting the weapon in a bag, or briefcase with other things -- and then forget it's there. If you wander into a courthouse or airport, even if you have a concealed permit -- you're gonna be in big trouble when the metal detector suddenly goes off![82] And, if you're thinking that this could never happen -- I can assure you that it happens all the time. Remember -- we're all just human!

"So", you ask. "Are there any defenses?"

Well, now that you've mentioned it, the answer is "yes". There is a defense which I like to term: "complete and utter stupidity". The court definition is a bit more legally precise, and is blandly referred to as a lack of knowledge, or lack of scienter.[83]   Since you were caught voluntarily placing a heavy metal object directly into a metal detector -- most people will probably come to realize that you did it innocently, rather than with a criminal intent. In other words, if you honestly forgot it was there, and can convince your friendly local prosecutor, or jury of that -- you will get out of it. Of course, you'll go through hell getting to that point. And, of course, this is normally subject to the assumption that you have no real criminal record, and aren't carrying drugs, other weapons, or a large amount of cash at the same time. Any of those additional factors would not be very helpful.

PEPPER SPRAY, TEAR-GAS, AND POCKET KNIVES:

While carrying concealed is generally illegal without a concealed permit, there are some exceptions to the general rules which were expanded 1n 1997 by the legislature. The exceptions allow you to carry a "common pocket knife", "self-defense chemical spray", "nonlethal stun gun", or other "nonlethal electric weapon or device". I'll explain the specifics for each one of these, shortly. Prior to this law, unless you had a concealed permit, you could only carry a "common pocketknife", or a "chemical defensive spray" containing no more than one half ounce of chemical.[84]   This has changed.

COMMON POCKETKNIVES:

A common pocketknife, according to Florida law, is not a "weapon", unless it is used as a deadly weapon.[85] Thus, anyone may carry a concealed "common pocketknife" without a permit. Until recently, this was a very confused area. The cases that interpreted the statute couldn't decide what the word "common" meant — and you took your chances whenever you had something even slightly unusual.[86] Federal law has been fairly clearcut,[87] and does not consider a "pocketknife" with a blade less than 2 ½ inches to be a "dangerous weapon".[88] In 1997 the confusion in Florida law was changed by an opinion by the Florida Supreme Court in L.B. v. State, 700 So.2d 370 (Fla. 1997).

Adopting a close version of the Attorney General's definition, and somewhat expanding on it, the Florida Supreme Court has held that a common pocketknife is not a "weapon" when it is a folding knife with a blade four inches or less. In fact, the Court noted there might be some instances where a pocketknife might still qualify as a "common" pocketknife if it had a blade length over four inches. In making the decision the Court stated:

> "Webster's defines "pocketknife" as "a knife with a blade folding into the handle to fit it for being carried in the pocket." From these definitions, we can infer that the legislature's intended definition of "common pocketknife" was: "A type of knife occurring frequently in the community which has a blade that folds into the handle and that can be carried in one's pocket." We believe that in the vast majority of cases, it will be evident to citizens and fact-finders whether one's pocketknife is a "common" pocketknife under any intended definition of that term. We need not be concerned with odd scenarios construing smaller but more expensive knives as "uncommon".

This definition should still exclude butterfly knives, automatic knives, or knives that do not fold in the traditional manner. A recent case held a 3 ½ inch bladed folding knife with a large finger guard, and notched combat-style grip still qualified as a weapon. J.D.L.R. v. State, 701 So.2d 626 (3DCA 1997). Thus, if it has significant features normally reserved to a combat type fighting knife — it may be considered a "weapon". My personal interpretation of that decision is that a finger guard is not a typical feature of a "common" pocketknife, and smacks more of a hunting knife, or combat style. Also, a common pocketknife may not be taken unto a school, school grounds, school bus stop, or school bus.

ELECTRIC & CHEMICAL WEAPONS:

Most pepper sprays have a maximum effective range of about ten feet. If the wind is blowing — make the proper adjustments, and make sure you aren't firing into a strong wind, or it may blow back on you. Make sure you buy something with at least 1.5 million SHU heat units — or it may be ineffective. Forget about percentages — it's the SHU's that count!

In 1997 the legislature amended some of the carrying restrictions concerning chemical and electronic weapons -- in favor of the ordinary citizen. You may now carry, for lawful self defense purposes, concealed or in the open, any "self-defense chemical spray". A "self-defense chemical spray" is a device carried solely for lawful self-defense, that is compact in size, is designed to be carried on or about a person, and contains no more than two (2) ounces of chemical.

You may also carry openly or concealed, for lawful self-defense, any "nonlethal electric weapon or device", including a stun gun, so long as the device does not shoot a dart or projectile This means that "Taser" type weapons still require a concealed permit!

Of course, you still can't have these weapons at schools, school buses, and school bus stops. I'll discuss these restrictions in Chapter Eight. However, the law makes no restrictions as to other places, although I wouldn't think you could get it into a jail, prison, or courthouse -- lawful or not.

QUESTION: Do you mean I can take a stun gun or pepper spray into a bar, concealed or in the open?

ANSWER: Yes, although I don't recommend you open carry as it will probably upset the world. However, the establishment can request that you get rid of it, and if you chose to ignore this request you have probably committed a misdemeanor trespass.[89]

One warning about these exciting exceptions to concealed and open carry laws — knowing and willful use of such weapons against a law enforcement officer engaged in the performance of his/her duties is a third degree felony. Moreover, unless the weapon is initially being carried for purposes of lawful self-defense — it's not covered under the statutory exception. Last, but not least, if you misuse the weapon for something other than lawful self-defense, you may still be prosecuted.

Before we get into the next section, let me add one point for general reference. Mace, tear gas, similar sprays, and most nonlethal electric weapons are not generally considered "dangerous" weapons.[90] This is because they are designed to temporarily incapacitate an opponent, rather than cause any permanent harm. If they do, it would normally be unintended. Thus, the use of mace, tear gas, pepper srpay, stun gun, etc., should not constitute the use of "deadly force", although it would certainly constitute the use of "non-deadly force". This will suddenly become enlightening when you get to Chapter Eleven, which concerns your right to self-defense.

OPEN CARRYING OF WEAPONS OTHER THAN FIREARMS:

Florida does not generally prohibit the open carrying of weapons (other than firearms, and lethal or non-defensive electric weapons) except on a school bus, at a school bus stop, or within 1000 feet of the real property that comprises a public or private elementary, middle, or secondary school.[91] More on this in Chapter Eight.

By "openly carry" I mean that the weapon is not concealed from ordinary view, and that anyone with moderate intelligence can see you have a weapon, if they bothered to take a look.[92]

Technically, this means you could carry a knife, machete, bow, cross-bow, sword, spear, nun-chuks, and almost anything else with you -- almost anywhere -- totally legal -- so long as they are not concealed. Amazing, huh?

QUESTION: You mean I can walk down the streets armed with a crossbow, or spear?

ANSWER: Yes, unless prohibited by ordinance. Although I don't suggest you try it with the more obvious of these weapons. Somehow, I don't think most people or police officers would appreciate you doing your personal impression of William Tell, or Attila the Hun -- no matter what the law says.

QUESTION: How about a stun gun?

ANSWER: Sure, as long as it's designed to be nonlethal, and is for defensive purposes -- unless it fires a dart, like a Taser. For now, dart firing electric weapons are treated like a firearm, and generally require a concealed permit, to carry.

QUESTION: Any place I couldn't open carry a weapon, other than a firearm, for sure?

ANSWER: Yes, schools, school buses, school bus stops. Read Chapter Eight for the low-down. Also, you're not getting in the courthouse with one, open or concealed. I assume that legal or not, the same applies to police stations, jails, and prisons — however, the legislature has left an inadvertent gap here, and restricted only concealed permit holders carrying concealed weapons pursuant to their permit.

IMPROPER EXHIBITION OF FIREARMS & WEAPONS:

The crime of improper exhibition of a firearm or other weapon is a normally a misdemeanor in Florida. It occurs when any person carrying a knife, sword cane, firearm, electric weapon, or any other weapon exhibits it to others in a rude, careless, angry, or threatening manner -- unless in necessary self-defense.[93] This does not mean that all you're doing is carrying it. Self-defense is a very involved topic, and is covered in detail in its own chapter. Therefore, I suggest you try not to figure it out until you get there. However, the normal framework of this particular crime is that you can't go threatening, frightening, or endangering people with the display of a weapon. If you do -- you've got problems, and will probably need my services.

In 1994 the Legislature made improper exhibition a third degree felony when done on any school bus, school bus stop, or within 1000 feet of the real property on which any school (excluded are nursery schools, colleges, and vocational schools) is located.[94] The law does not apply to <u>private</u> property within 1000 feet of a school, when the offender is there with permission.

There are also some tricky quirks to this statute that are covered in Chapter Eight. I suggest you read that chapter so you fully understand it.

DISCHARGING FIREARMS IN PUBLIC:

It is a first degree misdemeanor to discharge a firearm in any public place, from the right-of-way on any paved public road, or knowingly across any road or occupied premises. However, this would not apply if you were acting in lawful defense of self or property, if you were performing official duties requiring the discharge of a firearm, or if the public place or road was expressly approved for hunting by the State.

However, if you fire from a vehicle, and you know there's a person within 1000 feet of you -- hunting or not -- it's a second degree felony. Moreover, if you're the owner or driver of a vehicle, and you direct somebody else to fire from the vehicle -- it's a third degree felony.[95]

If you're wondering what all this means -- it means you can't fire a gun from inside, or on a vehicle unless in necessary self-defense.

DISCHARGING MACHINEGUNS:

First of all -- you can't have one without a special federal approval. Otherwise, you're looking at ten years in federal prison, and a very hefty fine. But assuming you're otherwise legal -- I don't suggest you fire any automatic weapon[96] unless it's at a range. Firing it almost anywhere else with the intent to injure persons or property is a first degree felony punishable by life imprisonment -- whether you hit anything or not.[97]

On the other hand, if you have the right to use deadly force -- your use of a machinegun is, with certain reservations, legal.[98] Again, it's not advised, especially as use of a firearm in the commission of certain felonies, where the firearm is capable of automatic or semi-automatic fire, and has a magazine capable of holding twenty or more center fire rounds requires very strict sentencing pursuant to a new legislative enactment in Chapter 99-12. This requires a mandatory minimum sentence of fifteen years if unfired, and 20 years if discharged. More on this in the self-defense chapter.

MACHINEGUNS, UNDERSIZED FIREARMS, AND OTHER NFA WEAPONS:

Possession of any automatic firearm; or a rifle with a barrel length of less than 16 inches (short-barreled rifle), or shotgun with a barrel length of less than 18 inches (short-barreled shotgun) is illegal under both State and Federal law, unless you have first obtained the tax stamp and transfer necessary under federal law. [99] Moreover, both rifles and shotguns must have an overall length of at least 26 inches. If you have a folding stock, lenth is measured from the tip of the barrel to the very end of the folding stock in its extended position, even if it can be fired without extension.[100] It is a second degree felony, as well as a federal crime to have such a firearm unless you have a federal Class III approval, and the special NFA tax stamp. When I talk about "NFA" weapons, I am speaking of those weapons regulated by the National Firearms Act, which falls under Internal Revenue Code jurisdiction, and can be found beginning at 26 USC 5801.

The most basic definition of a machinegun is under Florida law. In that sense, a machinegun is any firearm that shoots, or is designed to shoot more than one shot, automatically, by a single pull of the trigger.[101] If you're wondering why a "Hell Fire" equipped weapon doesn't qualify as such -- the "Hell Fire" causes multiple pulls of the trigger in extremely rapid succession -- thus although it mimics an automatic, it is still only "semi-automatic" because the trigger is being moved to accomplish the firing of each round.

Federal law is a lot tougher on what constitutes a machinegun because the federal definition includes the frames or receivers of machineguns, any parts designed to convert a weapon into machinegun, and any combination of parts from which a machinegun can be assembled.

Federal law also controls a number of other weapons and accessories under the National Firearms Act.

Some of the weapons and accessories that are a federal crime to possess under this Act, unless you are a dealer in this type weapon or have obtained a tax stamp and approval after completing the Form 4 application for transfer include: silencers and parts intended to fabricate a silencer, undersized firearms, destructive devices, cane guns, unhinged pen guns which fire a cartridge or tear gas by use of fixed ammunition ("fixed ammunition" is a single self-contained cartridge), and any pistol that is fitted for or with a shoulder stock -- unless the barrel length is over 16 inches, or if the weapon with stock has been placed on the "curio and relic" list by the Secretary of Treasury.[102]

If you want to know how to measure the length of your barrel to see if it's legal -- place a metal rod in the gun with the action closed, and mark where the rod exits the barrel. Measure that distance, and you have the official barrel length. 27 CFR 179.11

If you want to know why certain pen guns are legal, and others aren't, you must understand the interplay of definitions in federal law between "any other weapon",[103] and a "pistol":[104]

> "Any other weapon" means any weapon or device capable of being concealed on the person from which a shot can be discharged through the energy of an explosive.... Such term shall not include a pistol or revolver having a rifled bore...." 26 USC 5845 (e)

> Pistol: A weapon having "(b) a short stock designed to be gripped by one hand and at an angle to and extending below the line of the bore(s)." 27 CFR 178.11

If you read these two sections together you see that any weapon capable of being concealed is an "NFA" "any other weapon", unless excepted from the definition. One of the exceptions is if the weapon constitutes a "pistol" with a rifled bore. A pistol, to be a "pistol" under federal law, must also have a handle ("short stock") set at an angle to the barrel, and below the barrel. Therefore, when you buy a "hinged" pengun — the hinged portion is designed to be bent away from the barrel before it can fire. Thus, the hinged portion becomes the "handle" which is set at an angle to the barrel. Crazy, isn't it? Now, you know why you need a book to interpret this stuff!

Sorry, if I confused you. This stuff is often very complicated. To make it simpler, if any weapon that discharges a shell by an explosive charge can be concealed on your person, and that weapon does not have the normal configuration of a pistol or revolver -- is probably is "any other weapon" under federal law.

Similarly, a derringer that can be fired from within a concealing holster becomes "any other weapon" when placed in such a holster, because the angled grip extending from the barrel is no longer visible. Same thing with a gun rigged to be discharged from inside a briefcase. Also, there's a single shot pistol built into the handle of a knife which I've seen at some gun shows — its legal because the handle is set at an angle slightly below the barrel. Even that slight angled grip to the barrel brought it within the definition of a pistol, according an ATF ruling.

QUESTION: You mean if I have a derringer with a special wallet holster, I am illegal?

ANSWER: That's what BATF says! Once you put the two together you consider them as a "unit". The unit has now lost the "angled grip" it should have to be a pistol. You have a potential ten year federal felony! 26 USC 5871

QUESTION: You mean I can't fit a shoulder-stock to a regular pistol?

ANSWER: Absolutely not! It is no longer a "regular pistol" once you do. It falls under another definition of "any other weapon" because now it's a pistol designed to be fired from the shoulder, rather than by one hand. Another ten year federal "NFA" felony, unless it's exempted on the curio and relic list by the Secretary.

QUESTION: What if I cut-down my shotgun, and I'm a sixteenth of an inch too short?

ANSWER: Federal crime, and probable jail sentence. Mistakes are just your tough luck, and a possible reason to ask the judge for a more lenient sentence. On the other hand, you may have a shot at a defense that it was not "knowingly" or "willfully" done. Get a good lawyer!

QUESTION: Can I transport my legal machinegun just like any other firearm.

ANSWER: Within Florida, yes -- so long as you're federally legal. However, you are not covered under your Concealed Weapons Permit.

QUESTION: What else do I watch out for?

ANSWER: Well, anything unusual should be questioned, and anything too exotic looking might be something to stay away from unless you're really knowledgeable.

CHART ON LEGAL GUN & BARREL LENGTH:

Legal rifle length		Legal shotgun length	
barrel	overall	barrel	overall
16"	26"	18"	26"

USING A FIREARM WHILE UNDER THE INFLUENCE:

It is unlawful to have a <u>loaded</u> firearm in hand, or to fire such -- if you're under the influence of alcohol, or any harmful or illegal chemical substance to the extent your normal faculties are impaired.[105] If you do, it's a second degree misdemeanor, unless you're acting in lawful self-defense, or defense of your property. It will also cause the loss of your Concealed Weapons Permit, if you have one. Of course, if the firearm doesn't have ammunition in it — your still legal — but definitely stupid.

"Normal faculties" doesn't mean you'rc "drunk". Normal faculties is a lesser standard normally associated with DUI, and means that your coordination, ability to see, speak, judge distances, perform ordinary tasks, or make decisions is affected to an extent that these functions are noticeably interfered with. If you have a "buzz", you are certainly under the influence, and maybe drunk, as well. If you need to try harder to concentrate -- same thing. If you've just had a couple, and it has relaxed you, but nothing more -- you're not under the influence in the legal sense, because although all alcohol has had some effect -- it hasn't yet affected your "normal faculties".

If a law enforcement officer has probable cause to believe you were using a firearm while under the influence, he can require you to take a breath test for alcohol, and a urine test for drugs. If you caused death or serious injury to anyone -- he may take blood, and take it by force if you refuse.

A blood alcohol reading of .10 percent or greater is evidence of being under the influence of alcohol to the extent your normal faculties are impaired. Less than .05 percent means you're presumed to be fine. Anywhere in between means "it depends". Although the DUI standard has changed to .08 percent as the presumed level of intoxication since January 1, 1994 -- a .10 will still apply for this firearms offense.[106]

Personally, I don't think you should be walking around with a loaded firearm if you are anything other than stone cold sober, unless somebody or something is coming at you. Otherwise, it's too damn. risky.[107]

SHOOTING AT VEHICLES, VESSELS & STRUCTURES:

The deliberate or reckless shooting, or throwing of any projectile or other hard object which could produce great bodily harm, at or into any building, whether occupied or not, or at any boat, train, aircraft, bus, or any other vehicle which is occupied or being used by any person -- is a second degree felony.[108] This is the statute that juveniles are usually charged with when they throw rocks from bridges, and overpasses -- and miss. If they hit anybody, add aggravated battery and possibly murder to the list. Anything that can produce serious injury qualifies. A rock, piece of debris, shooting with a firearm or bow, etc. Very dangerous stuff -- especially if the vehicle is moving, and adds its velocity to the impact.

SELF-PROPELLED KNIVES:

It is a first degree misdemeanor to manufacture, sell, or possess any spring knife, or "self-propelled" knife -- which is a device that propels a knifelike blade, generally by use of a coiled spring, compressed gas, or elastic.[109] Bows, cross-bows, and spearguns are excluded from this definition if they discharge a bolt, dart, or arrow.

POSSESSION BY CONVICTED FELON:

Under Florida law any person convicted of a felony in this, or any other state, or of a crime that would be considered a felony in Florida[110], or a federal felony, is considered a "convicted felon", and such a person cannot possess, own, or have in his/her care or custody any firearm or electric weapon, without first having his right to own and possess such being restored by executive clemency, or by a proceeding to remove the disability under federal law. A convicted felon is also forbidden from carrying concealed, any weapon whatsoever, including chemical sprays. Violation is a second degree felony, unless you qualify as a "violent career criminal". If you do, it's a first degree felony with a mandatory minimum 15 year sentence.[111]   Even juveniles may qualify as violent career criminals, and are subject to the mandatory sentence if prosecuted in adult court. F.S. 790.235

Juveniles who do not qualify as "violent career criminals" under F.S. 790.235, get a break when they become an adult. Any "convicted felon" status disability expires, unless the prior conviction was in adult court vs. juvenile court.[112] However, their prior juvenile adjudications can still be counted to later qualify them for "violent career criminal" status if they don't clean-up their act.

Federal law on convicted felons is somewhat different because it adds to the prohibitions the possession or ownership of ammunition. Since ammunition includes any component (ie: a single dummy shell would do, or even an empty casing) — it can be a real trap for the unwary.

> QUESTION: My boyfriend, and I live together. He is a convicted felon, and wants a gun in the house. Can I buy it for him, if I keep it.

ANSWER: No. If you're buying it "for him", it's a second degree felony, and you're probably an accessory.

QUESTION: How about if I really just want it for me, and not for him.

ANSWER: First, he should not have access to the firearm. You should keep it on your person, and when not on your person, it should be kept locked somewhere that he does not have either the key, or combination.   This is still somewhat risky, but technically legal.   Also,   don't leave   any ammunition lying around -- otherwise he's still subject to serious problems. Remember, even if it's yours -- he might be charged with "constructive possession". That means that he has knowledge of where the firearm is located, and has the legal ability to control it, as well. This gets very tricky, and is not worth the risk.

QUESTION: How about an antique firearm?

ANSWER: An "antique firearm" is not considered a firearm unless used in the commission of a crime, therefore it is legal for a convicted felon to have such a weapon (when not on probation) so long as it is not concealed. Same thing for a bow, or crossbow, etc. Just stay away from firearms, electric weapons, and any concealed weapon.

USE OR POSSESSION OF A FIREARM DURING THE COMMISSION OF A FELONY:

The mere carrying of a firearm during the commission of a felony, is a separate felony of the third degree under Florida law.   That means that nobody even needs to see it -- only that you have it. If you display it, use it, or threaten its use -- it's a second degree felony.[113] Moreover, whatever felony you were involved with is generally increased one degree, and certain felonies, including most defined as a "forcible felony" receive a "mandatory minimum" sentence of three (3) years -- which means that the judge must impose that sentence, as the absolute minimum of prison time, even if he doesn't want to.[114]   You will see how this has a very "chilling" effect on your right to self-defense later when we discuss aggravated assault.

And, if you committed the crime while being armed with a semi-automatic with a high capacity clip, which is a box magazine capable of holding more than 20 centerfire cartridges, or if you were armed with a machine gun -- make it an fifteen (15) year mandatory minimum.[115]

USE OF BULLETPROOF VEST WHILE COMMITTING FELONY:

Any person who, while possessing a firearm, commits or attempts to commit a murder, sexual battery, robbery, burglary, kidnapping, arson, aggravated battery, aggravated assault, escape, or aircraft piracy -- and has the nerve to wear a bulletproof vest in furtherance of the crime -- is guilty of a third degree felony. Again, this is a very good law unless you're acting in self-defense, and overstep what you can or cannot do.

ARMOR PIERCING OR SPECIALITY AMMUNITION:

F.S. 790.31 governs the "Florida version" of what is, and is not allowed in most ammunition for firearms. Under the Florida statute an "armor-piercing bullet" is one with an inner core of steel or other metal of equivalent hardness (not lead), and a truncated cone (ie: a cut-off tip) which is designed for use in a handgun as an armor or metal piercing bullet. If it isn't designed for a handgun — it doesn't meet the definition.

Other Florida "no-no's" under F.S. 790.31 include the following list of exotics:

a.   "Exploding bullet" — is one that is designed to detonate by use of an explosive or deflagrant (ie: burning agent) contained or attached to the bullet, and can be fired from any firearm.

b.   "Dragon's breath shotgun shell" which is one that is solely designed to spew a flame or fireball (not a tracer — but simulates a flamethrower), and contains exothermic pyrophoric misch metal as the projectile.

c.   "Bolo shell" which is any shell that expels two or more metal balls connected by a solid metal wire, and can be fired in a firearm.

d.   "Flechette shell" means any shell with two or more pieces of fin-stabilized metal wires or solid dart-type projectiles, that can be fired in a firearm.

Under the Florida statute it is a third degree felony to sell, offer for sale, or deliver any of these five types of ammunition. Also, if you merely possess armor piercing ammo when it is loaded into a handgun, you are also guilty of a third degree felony. Same thing for the other four types of exotics — except they can't be loaded into any type firearm, not just a handgun. If you possess any with the intent to use it in the commission of a crime, loaded or not, it's a second degree felony — 15 years!

Of course, the statute excepts law enforcement use, and sale to law enforcement agencies.

Federal law is a bit different because it doesn't cover purchase, possession, use, or sale by private individuals — unless in the commission of a crime.[116] On the other hand, federal licensees (legal gun dealers or "FFL") are strictly controlled on what they can sell. To find out how the definitions work in federal land — here we go:

a.   "Armor piercing" is any projectile or its core which may be used in a handgun which is made entirely of steel, iron, brass, bronze, beryllium, copper, depleted uranium, or a combination of tungsten alloys, or

A full jacketed projectile larger than .22 caliber which is designed and intended for use in a handgun, and whose jacket weighs more than 25% of the total weight of the projectile.

Excluded from the definition of armor piercing are shotgun shot required by game regulations for hunting, frangible projectiles designed for target shooting (ie: breaks up on way to target), and projectiles which are determined by BATF to be used for sporting purposes, or industrial purposes.

If you noticed, <u>lead</u> is not one of the prohibited metals under Florida or Federal law. Also, you need not worry about federal law unless you are an FFL, or intend to use the ammunition in the commission of a felony.

QUESTION: I have some old 7:62 x 39 steel core ammo for my SKS. I heard it was illegal to shoot it?

ANSWER: Nope. It's fine unless loaded into a handgun. However, a dealer couldn't sell it to you.

QUESTION: I've got some handgun ammo that is supposed to "explode" like a shotgun shell when it hits someone. Isn't that an illegal exploding bullet?

ANSWER: Nope. An "exploding" bullet must actually have some chemical or such to make it explode or incinerate upon contact. The type of round your talking about is quite common, and works purely from the force of impact. Normally, you're talking about something like "<u>safety shot</u>" which contains a number of small pellets that <u>disburse</u> upon impact. Other bullets may be designed to fragment upon impact, with the idea of creating a greater wound channel — thus stopping the assailant before he stops you.

QUESTION: Why call it "safety shot"?

ANSWER: Since these rounds fragment, or disburse -- they lose momentum quicker, and therefore won't generally penetrate walls if you miss. Thus, you don't hit something or someone you didn't intend to. Lots of pros and cons — buy a book on ammunition.

ALTERED OR REMOVED SERIAL NUMBERS:

It is a state and federal felony to knowingly remove or alter a serial number on any firearm, or otherwise attempt to disguise it's identification.[117] It is also a felony to knowingly possess, sell, or deliver such a firearm, and if you find a firearm with the serial numbers missing, or partially or completely filed, you should call your local police department, and turn it in. First, because it's a crime to have it. Second, because you are on notice that the gun is probably stolen -- and it's also a state and federal felony to possess or sell a stolen firearm.[118]

DESTRUCTIVE DEVICES:

A "destructive device" under Florida law encompasses both the state and federal definitions.[119] These are many. In its most basic definition it is any bomb, grenade, mine, rocket, missile, or similar device that contains an explosive, incendiary, or poison gas which is designed or constructed to explode, and is capable of causing bodily harm or property damage. It also includes any breakable container filled with an explosive, incendiary, explosive or expanding gas designed or constructed to explode due to its content, and capable of causing bodily harm or property damage. This is usually a "Molotov cocktail".

It also includes any weapon with a barrel diameter over one half inch capable of expelling a projectile by means of an explosive -- other than a legal sized shotgun[120], line-throwing device (rescue), or signaling device. Ammunition for destructive devices are included in the definition of a "destructive device". A 1994 treasury ruling outlawed three shotguns, the Striker, USAS-12, and Streetsweeper -- unless they are registered under the National Firearms Act, just like a machinegun. The reason is that the federal definition of destructive device includes any "weapon" that expels a projectile by means of an explosive having a barrel bore of more than one half inch, except a shotgun or shotgun shell the Secretary of Treasury finds is generally recognized as particularly suitable for sporting purposes. The Secretary found that these particular guns had no legitimate sporting purpose, and were really riot and combat weapons.

I also note that the federal statute makes the definition of destructive device a bit clearer than the Florida statute. That's because of the following language concerning the required status as a "weapon" before it becomes a destructive device:

> "The term 'destructive device' shall not include any device which is neither designed or redesigned for use as a weapon; any device, although originally designed for use as a weapon, which is redesigned for use as a signaling, pyrotechnic, line throwing, safety, or similar device . . . or any other device which the Secretary finds is not likely to be used as a weapon, or is an antique . . . ."

Thus, you now can understand why a potato cannon is not normally a destructive device. Why? Because it is not something "designed" as a "weapon". Of course, under the Florida definition — if you use it as a weapon — it becomes a destructive device under Florida law.

Whatever!

SWITCHBLADE KNIFE:

It is not illegal to possess a switchblade knife in Florida, although many other states prohibit them. It is not illegal to have a switchblade in your vehicle, securely encased. However, if you have one concealed on your person, and it's not covered under the exceptions in F.S. 790.25 -- you do need a concealed permit.

On the other hand it is a federal felony for anyone to sell or distribute these knives, unless they were manufactured in the state of sale. Furthermore, it is a federal felony for an individual to transport them into another state, on any federal waters outside of a state's jurisdiction, and on Indian land. There are other restrictions — but this should do.[121]

Just as an aside, you might like to know that switchblades were extensively used as a utility knife by women in the 1800's, and early 1900's -- because their long fingernails would break when opening ordinary pocketknives. They also served as a "safety" knife, as they could be opened with one hand. Thus, if one hand was trapped, or pinned -- the knife could still be opened to help cut you loose.

ASSAULT WEAPONS:

After a bitter fight, Congress incorporated the Assault Weapons Ban into the 1994 Crime Bill. Of course, the old definition of an "assault weapon" is an automatic or select fire weapon that can be fired in bursts like a machinegun, suitable for the military, and usually including a bayonet mount. However, the ban makes its own definitions, and makes it a crime to purchase, transfer, or possess "assault" firearms manufactured or imported after the passage date of the law, unless the firearm is specifically exempted. The same goes for magazines, feed strips, and drums which have the capability of holding over ten rounds -- even if they are for pistols. The primary question will be whether they were imported or manufactured prior to the ban becoming law. Firearms and magazines that are manufactured or imported after the Act becomes law -- are required to have the date clearly incorporated into their serial number. So, look before you buy![122]

If your possession of such a firearm is legal, then you may legally transfer the firearm to another person without any further paperwork, as long as that person has no legal disability. Since I'm sure you want to know all the details, the ban is extensively discussed in Chapter Ten.

USE OF BANGSTICKS:

The use of a bangstick or powerhead for self-protection in the salt water areas within State jurisdiction is generally permitted, although the taking of any marine life thereby is strictly prohibited.[123] In other words, unless one of our finny friends has definite plans on having you for dinner, don't use it.

Moreover, you should make sure that the powerhead is permanently attached to a shaft with an overall length of not less than four feet, so you don't fall within the definition of "any other weapon" under federal law -- which, as we just discussed a few sections ago, is very illegal.[124]

Use of powerheads within National and State Parks is another matter, and will not generally be permitted.

QUESTION: How could a bangstick become "any other

weapon" under the NFA?

ANSWER: Well, it's only real purpose is a "weapon" —
            against sharks. If it can be concealed on the
            person it then qualifies as "any other weapon"
            since it's not otherwise excepted. The Revenue
            Ruling in the last endnote said if it's four foot long
            with a permanent shaft — it's fine because it really
            can't be concealed at that length. So, if you want
            to play it safe — do it the way they tell you.

ARMED TRESPASS:

Trespassing on the property of another while in possession of a
firearm, loaded or not --is a third degree felony under F.S. 810.09.
Basically, a trespass occurs if you go uninvited onto enclosed or posted
lands; if you enter or remain in a structure or conveyance without having
any express or implied invitation to do so; or if having been warned to
leave, you refuse to do so.[125]

While I have found no Florida cases on the subject, there are many
instances in which you go into a store, or shopping center -- and they have
a sign posted saying "no firearms permitted". The next question you
must face is whether you commit a trespass by going in the store. If so,
then you've also committed an "armed trespass", which is a third degree
felony.

My personal opinion is that your going into such a store or
shopping mall is not a trespass just because they post a sign saying "no
firearms". Again, that's a personal interpretation. A court could call me
wrong, and if you want to play it safe — obey the sign.

On the other hand, if you do follow my interpretation, and they
asked you to leave, and you refused -- that would be another story, and
you'd be in serious trouble. However, the store wants your business, and
you are legally an invitee. If they had a guard posted at the mall entrance,
and asked you if you were armed -- and you lied -- again, I think you have
a problem. But, in essence, they really are only posting these things to
protect themselves from a liability standpoint in case something happens.
That way, you get sued -- they don't!

Since the offense of trespass by an invitee would require a warning, and a refusal to depart my opinion is that you can't legally "refuse" until someone asks you to leave. Then, it's time to swallow your pride, and exit very quickly, and very politely. If the wife, and kids are somewhere else in the mall -- ask security if you can locate them before you leave, or, if not -- ask if they'll make an announcement. Don't push your luck if they're reluctant or refuse. Just get the hell out of there, pronto! If the wife or kids will be confused -- try bribing some honest-looking passerby outside the mall to notify them. All this is alot better than an arrest, and a third degree felony on your record!

LICENSED PRIVATE SECURITY GUARDS:

Chapter 493, Florida Statutes, governs the use of firearms by private investigative, security, and repossession services. The regulations pertaining to this Chapter would take a separate book, so I'll be brief. First, you cannot carry a firearm or weapon as part of your duties without a "G" license. If you do, and get caught -- you'll probably lose your license for at least five years. You'll also be committing a first degree misdemeanor.[126]

Security personnel with a Concealed Weapons Permit may be able to legally carry a firearm without committing a crime in their private lives, but professionally, unless they have also have a "G" license, are required to carry a firearm as part of their duties, and are doing so in connection with their duties -- they will be in serious trouble with the Licensing Division of the Department of State, will be committing a misdemeanor, and will be a walking civil liability case, if anything happens. This is because there are very stringent training requirements to obtain and maintain a "G" license, and those who don't meet these requirements are deemed to be "unqualified" to carry a weapon while on duty.

The type of firearm which can be carried is set forth in F.S. 493.6115(6), and appears in this chart. Do not load .357 ammo!

CLASS	C	CC	D	M	MB	MA
.380	X					X
.38	X	X	X	X	X	X
.357	X	X	X	X	X	X

9 mm	X					X

Prohibited ammo for security guards:

a.   Glasser, Mag-Safe, etc. pre-fragmented type bullets
b.   exploding bullets
c.   full metal jacket
d.   teflon coated (ktw) or other armor-piercing
e.   full wadcutters & reloads (except for range use)
f.   .357 — use .38

CHAPTER EIGHT

LAWS CONCERNING CHILDREN

Whenever I mention children, the first thing I think of is airguns, fireworks, and where the heck should I put my gun to make sure they don't get hold of it. Children, the younger the more common, have a bad habit of playing with things they shouldn't. If they get hold of a loaded firearm -- the results can be devastating. More importantly, when it happens, it happens so quickly that there are only seconds to counter the potential disaster. School shootings don't help much, either. To counter this tragic situation, the Florida legislature has gone a bit too far -- and the federal government, as usual -- has gone off the wall. Whatever the merits or demerits of these laws -- the first part of this chapter should educate you on what to be aware of in this area.

LAWFUL AGE TO POSSESS FIREARMS OR AMMUNITION:

The passage of the Youth Handgun Safety Amendment to the 1994 federal Crime Bill[127] made it a federal crime for anyone to sell, deliver, or otherwise transfer to a juvenile (ie: person under 18 years of age) a handgun, or ammunition suitable only for use in a handgun. This means loaded, or unloaded. This means a gift, a sale, just loaning the darn thing, or temporarily handing it over for a "look-see". This applies to parents, uncles, aunts, friends, relatives, scout masters, and any almost every other form of life on the planet, except for firearms dealers. For firearms dealers -- it's still 21 years of age. The exceptions under the statute are a "temporary transfer" for use during:

a.   In the course of ranching, or farming at the residence of the juvenile, or

b.   In the course of ranching, or farming at a location where the juvenile has the permission of the property owner or lessee, or

c.   during target practice, hunting, or a course of instruction on the safe and lawful use of firearms, or

    d.   in the course of employment.

On top of these restrictions, there are additional requirements. The additional requirements that must be met while the permitted activities are being performed. These additional restrictions are as follows:

    a.   The juvenile must have the prior written consent of a parent or guardian. The written consent must be kept on the juveniles person at all times he is in possession of the handgun or ammunition (during the permitted activity), and the parent or guardian who gave permission, must not have a legal disability that would make it illegal for that parent or guardian to possess a firearm.

    b.   The handgun must be transported unloaded, in a locked container, directly to and from the permitted activity. It must thereafter be returned to an adult.

    c.   If the activity is ranching or farming, then such must be done at the direction of an adult who does not have a legal disability that would make it illegal for that person to possess a firearm.

Now, if you thought that wasn't enough, here's another doozie. Subsection (D) only allows a juvenile to use a handgun in defense of the juvenile, or another person, if it's against an "intruder" inside the residence of the juvenile, or a residence in which the juvenile is a guest!

Do you know what that supposedly means? It means that if Dad suddenly goes nuts, and begins killing the family, and the kid grabs a handgun to try to stop it -- he's committed a crime! If mom is bloody on the floor, and gives it to the kid because she couldn't use it herself -- she's facing a year in federal prison -- assuming she survives. Why? Because Daddy is not an "intruder". He lives there! Moreover, if it's at the office, in the car, etc. -- same stupid result. Your Congress in action! Yay, team!

Anyway, since we're all sick of federal law by now, let's get into Florida law. Don't get too excited -- we've still got some more federal law to go over later in this chapter. It never ends.

FLORIDA LAWS PERTAINING TO MINORS:

In Florida, it is unlawful for anyone to sell, lend, or give a person under the age of 18 years any weapon, whatsoever, except an ordinary pocketknife -- unless a parent (guardian) gives permission. A violation is a first degree misdemeanor for weapons, and a third degree felony for firearms.[128] A "dealer in arms" cannot sell to a person under 18 years of age -- even with permission, although he can legally sell to an adult, who may then transfer it to the child, with permission from a parent.[129]

A 1996 amendment to F.S. 790.22 makes it illegal for a minor under 16 years to possess a BB gun, air or gas operated gun, or electric weapon unless such is in the presence of, and under the supervision of an adult who acts with consent of one of the minor's parents. It is a second degree misdemeanor for the adult to knowingly and willfully permit such possession.

If it's a firearm, then it's illegal for a minor under 18 years to possess it unless:

a.   Engaged in lawful hunting, and is
      1.   At least 16 years old, or
      2.   Under 16, and is supervised by adult

b.   Engaged in lawful recreational shooting or marksmanship, and is
      1.   At least 16 years, or
      2.   Under 16 and supervised by adult acting with consent of minor's parent or guardian.

c.   Firearm is unloaded, and being transported by minor directly to or from an event authorized by this statute.
d.   Firearm is unloaded, and possessed at child's home.

PENALTIES & CHART FOR CHILD VIOLATIONS:

Any parent, guardian, or other adult who is responsible for the minor who knowingly and willfully permits the minor to have a firearm in violation of this section — commits a third degree felony!   The other possible penalty for minors and parents are in the following chart:

WITH FIREARM	Type offense	Sentence to jail	community service	weapon	driver license
first offense	misd.	up to 3 days	minimum 100 hours	forfeit	up to 1 year loss
second offense	3d felony	up to 15 days	100 -250 hours	forfeit	up to 2 year loss
1st offense & a crime	1st misd.	15 days minimum	minimum 100 hours	forfeit	up to 1 year loss
2d offense & a crime	3d felony	21 days minimum	100 - 250 hours	forfeit	up to 2 year loss
adult in charge	knowingly and willfully permits child to possess firearm in violation of law is third degree felony.				
parent or guardian	same as above, except may also be required to attend parenting classes, and do community service with child.				
VIOLATIONS WHERE AIRGUN OR ELECTRIC WEAPON ONLY					
child	possible delinquency proceeding under F.S. 985				
adult in charge	second degree misdemeanor				

Other recent additions to the statute (Chapter 99-284) permit a child who is taken into custody for possession of a firearm on school property to be detained for up to 21 days for psychological, drug, and medical examination in the discretion of the court.   A further addition is that when the violation involves underage possession of a firearm, and a separate violation of another criminal statute — community control can be imposed, and the court may also order the parents or guardians of the child to pay restitution for any damage caused, unless the parents/guardians can show they made a diligent and good faith effort to prevent such conduct.

In closing, what this law doesn't say, is it's obvious that a number of weapons can be possessed by a child <u>under sixteen (16)</u> without supervision -- if they have permission to have the weapon in the first place. Those would include everything <u>but</u> firearms, airguns, and electric weapons. Thus, knives, hatchets, machetes, bows, etc. -- are otherwise legal if not concealed, are obtained with permission of the parent, and are not in violation of any of the laws pertaining to schools, school sponsored events, school bus stops, and school buses.

QUESTION: So, can I buy my kid an air rifle if he is 12 years old?

ANSWER: Sure. But if you let him use it or possess it when you or another adult is not around (until the age of 16 years) -- you're guilty of a misdemeanor.

QUESTION: What if he's 16 years old.

ANSWER: That changes things a little. Now he can possess and use the airgun without supervision.

QUESTION: What about a real rifle -- a 22 caliber?

ANSWER: Well, from 16 until 18 years — he can have it unloaded at home. If he's taking it anywhere, it must be kept unloaded, and be in transport directly to or from lawful recreational shooting, or lawful hunting. Nowhere else! If you let him do otherwise — you've committed a felony!

QUESTION: What if my wife and I disagree? She says "no" -- I say "yes".

ANSWER: Your kid can have the weapon or firearm, but your wife will make both your lives miserable.

QUESTION: So, if I can buy it -- can he keep it in his room?

ANSWER: Yes, if it is unloaded, and is not a handgun.

QUESTION: What about a hunting knife, or bow and arrows?

109

ANSWER: If a parent, or guardian allows the child to have it
-- the child may have it at any age: 3, 5, 10, 14
years old -- whatever age they allow. Once the
child reaches 18 years of age -- the "child" can
purchase any type of weapon, on his own,
including handguns -- but cannot purchase the
handgun from a federally licensed dealer until 21.

QUESTION: What if the kid wants a weapon, and the wife and
I refuse to give permission.

ANSWER: If a parent or guardian doesn't give permission,
then the child cannot legally obtain any weapon,
other than a common pocketknife, until he reaches
18 years of age.

QUESTION: What happens at 18 years of age?

ANSWER: The "child" becomes an "adult", for most
purposes, and may legally buy any weapon,
including a handgun, although he cannot buy a
handgun from a federally licensed dealer.

QUESTION: What if his grandfather bequested him an antique
handgun?

ANSWER: Interesting question. It appears that this was an
inadvertent loophole left by both Florida and
federal legislators. An "antique firearm" is not a
"firearm" unless being used in the commission of
a crime. Even the definition of a "handgun" under
federal law must still be a "firearm", thus
excluding antique firearms. It's obviously not a
BB gun or air gun. It's not a "firearm". I guess
it's OK for the kid to have it until somebody gets
around to changing the law, so long as it's given
to the child with the permission of a parent. Still,
you could become a "test case" on this one.

STORAGE OF LOADED FIREARMS:

In this day and age, it should be easy to keep firearms away from children -- but anyone who has been around kids can testify that they can get into anything -- sometimes so fast, it's scary. In order to cut your losses, the Legislature has enacted laws making it a crime to leave a loaded gun accessible to children under the age of 16 years[130] except under certain circumstances. If it's unloaded -- you don't have to worry about these statutes.[131] Thus, the storing of a loaded firearm within the reach or easy access of a minor child under the age of sixteen, where the person knows, or should know, the minor is likely to gain access to it without lawful permission or supervision is a felony of the third degree if the minor obtains the firearm and uses it to inflict injury or death upon himself or any other person.[132] If no injury occurs, but the minor still gains access to the firearm -- it's a second degree misdemeanor -- only if the minor unlawfully possesses it in a public place, or displays it anywhere, in a "rude, careless, angry, or threatening manner". Of course, if the child was in presence and under the supervision of an adult, at the time (and it's one of our wonderful federally permitted activities), it's also fine, unless the adult was otherwise culpably negligent under F.S. 784.05

You should know that this law would not impose criminal liability when the firearm was stored in a securely locked box/container, or in a location which a reasonable person would believe to be secure, or if the firearm had a trigger lock, or mounted firearm combination lock. It also would not apply if the person who left the firearm should not have reasonably known that a minor was likely to gain access to the firearm without the permission or supervision of a parent or person having charge of the minor, or if it resulted from an unlawful entry by any person. And, if the firearm is being carried by an adult on his body, or within such proximity to his person that he could retrieve, and use it as easily and quickly as if he carried it on his body ("readily accessible for immediate use") -- it's also legal.

QUESTION: What if my sister's kids come over, and I'm a bachelor. I always keep my gun in a bureau by my bed?

ANSWER: Assuming they don't sneak in the back door, and you have time to take some security precautions, it may be reasonable to contemplate that the kids may go searching around. Thus, unloading the weapon, putting on a trigger lock, or locking it in a container -- instantly take you off the hook. If you want to be a bit riskier it becomes a jury question of whether you acted reasonably, or not. Obviously, if they get hold of the gun -- you have a potential legal problem.

QUESTION: What if I'm driving my kids in the car, and I've got my loaded gun in a closed console next to me.

ANSWER: In my opinion, you're legal as long as you're in the vehicle, you're in the driver's seat, and the console is closed. That's because the statute exempts situations where you are carrying the firearm on your body, "or within such close proximity thereto that he can retrieve and use it as easily and quickly as if he carried it on his body." F.S. 790.174(1).

CIVIL PROBLEMS IF THE KIDS GET TO IT:

If a child under the age of 18 years willfully or recklessly destroys or injures the property of another -- the parent or parents he lives with are legally responsible for the actual amount of damages the child causes. This is pursuant to F.S. 741.24. If you were negligent in leaving the firearm in a place where a child could reasonably have been anticipated to get hold of it -- you are probably going to be held civilly liable for any damages caused by that child's use of the firearm -- including the death or injury of somebody else. Conceivably, you might even be subject to a manslaughter or culpable negligence prosecution.

Obviously, the way to get around this is to buy one of the many devices available to keep a loaded gun ready for use -- but safe. There are a number of small gun boxes or safes that have a lock that opens by pushing a combination of push buttons. Since it can be opened by "feeling" the buttons -- it can be accessed in total darkness, right next to your bed. If you have kids -- this is really what you need.

If you just want a safe gun locker -- many are available at almost any sporting goods store, gun shops, gun shows, and even at K-Mart. Prices range from really cheap -- to really expensive, and fit all purposes and pocketbooks. If you keep a number of firearms, you might want to keep them in a really secure gun locker -- because the majority of illegal guns were stolen by teenagers during burglaries from honest owners just like you. Then the guns are used against the rest of us. Be responsible -- make sure your guns are safe from kids -- and safe from theft.

As far as trigger locks go — I am not a great believer in them, as I think a lock box, or gun safe is far superior. To me, a trigger lock is solely a "storage solution", and not a very good one. A stored gun doesn't have to be loaded — and shouldn't be. Moreover, if you have a trigger lock on a self-defense gun — you are going to be dead before you get it unlocked. There are some recent improvements on "electronically keyed", and other push-button mechanisms installed directly on the gun such a "Safe-T-Lock" mechanism — but if that's your answer to keeping the gun where it can be found — I think you need a better solution.

GUN FREE SCHOOL ZONES ACT -- PART TWO:

Well, just as I promised, we're back in federal land. Congress has a bad habit of passing laws that should really be reserved for the decision of the individual states. I already described in the first chapter how the United States Supreme Court decided that this law was unconstitutional, but Congress didn't really care about such minor problems, and reenacted it, again. My best guess is that the reenacted law, 18 USC 922(q), should be just as unconstitutional as the last one -- but nobody really knows what the courts will do, especially federal courts. So, here's how this wonderful law works:

In brief, the law makes it a federal crime punishable by up to five years imprisonment to knowingly possess a firearm in a "school zone" unless you meet certain exceptions. A "school zone" is defined as the grounds of any public, private, or parochial elementary or secondary school — or within 1000 feet of such. The exceptions are any of the following:

1. You've got a concealed permit
2. The gun is not loaded, and is in a locked container , or locked firearm rack in a motor vehicle

3.   You're on private property, not part of the school
4.   It's for use in a program approved by a school in the school zone (not necessarily at the school)
5.   You're a security guard under contract with a school in the school zone
6.   You're a law enforcement officer acting as such
7.   The gun is unloaded, and you're traversing school grounds for the purpose of legal access to hunting land, if the school authority has authorized such.

FLORIDA SCHOOL ZONE LAWS:

In 1997 the legislature passed another law[133] affecting school type situations which amended F.S. 790.115. It sounds something like the federal law we just discussed, but has very few similarities when you fully examine it. You should be aware that it has two key sections that are very dissimilar -- one devoted to unlawful "display" of firearms and other weapons, and another devoted to mere "possession". A violation of either is a third degree felony unless you are a concealed permit holder. There is a third section that deals with unlawful discharge of weapons which is a second degree felony. Anyway — here's how it works:

The first subsection (1) deals with unlawful exhibition of weapons and firearms, and does not pertain to mere possession. It makes it illegal to display any sword, sword cane, firearm, electric weapon, destructive device, or other weapon including a razor blade, box cutter, or knife, including "common pocketknife" in a "rude, careless, angry, or threatening manner, not in lawful self-defense, and in the presence of one or more persons:
1.   On the grounds or facilities of any school
2.   On any school bus stop
3.   On any school bus
4.   At any school sponsored event (even off school property)
5.   Or, within 1000 feet of the grounds of any elementary, middle, or secondary school

during school hours, or during the time of a school sanctioned school activity. This section does not apply to exhibition of a firearm or weapon on private property within 1000 feet of school grounds if such is done by the owner, or by a person who has been authorized, licensed, or invited by the owner to his property.

The second subsection (2) deals with mere possession, and forbids a person from "willfully and knowingly" possessing any firearm, electric weapon, destructive device, or other weapon, including a razor blade, box cutter, or knife, including common pocketknife, except as authorized in support of school sanctioned activities, on the property of any school, school bus stop, school sponsored event, or school bus. The definition of a school is confusingly expanded to include preschool, elementary, middle, junior high, secondary, post secondary, and vocational schools -- public or private. There is also no restriction as to time of day. In other words, it doesn't matter whether the school is in session, or not. There is fortunately no "1000 foot" prohibition, so if you're one foot off the school grounds, and you've got a weapon on you -- this section of the statute does not affect you.

As to the exceptions to this subsection which will make it lawful to possess a firearm or a weapon (not unlawfully display), here they are:

1.   To a firearms program, class, or function that has been approved in advance by the principal or chief administrative officer of the school

2.   To a vocational school having a firearms training range

3.   In a vehicle pursuant to F.S. 790.25(5) — ie: securely encased or not readily accessible. However, you should know that the legislature made a very bad mistake here, and receded somewhat from our "preemption" law[134] by permitting a school district to adopt written and published policies that waive this exemption for purposes of student and campus parking privileges.

4.   The penalties of this subsection also do not apply to concealed permit holders. Such persons are punished as provided in F.S. 790.06(12), which makes a violation of that particular subsection of 790.06 a second degree misdemeanor -- except that a license holder who unlawfully discharges a weapon or firearm on school property as prohibited by this subsection commits a second degree felony. As I stated in the chapter on

concealed permits — this "should" mean that you can possess on school grounds pursuant to that subsection -- but I strongly advise against it. It isn't worth being a "test case".

The third section of this statute deal with the discharge of a weapon or firearm while in violation of the possession prohibitions of this section, unless discharged in lawful self defense, or for other lawful purpose. As previously stated, such is a second degree felony.

A fourth section of the statute deals with safe storage of firearms, and really is a duplication of F.S. 790.174 with some gloss. We already covered it when we discussed that statute.

A new enactment in Chapter 99-284 also provides that a child who possesses a firearm on school property may be held for up to 21 days for observation and treatment

QUESTION: OK, I'm a law-abiding citizen walking down the street with my self-defense chemical spray legally clipped to the outside of my purse. I suddenly see a school, 999 feet away. I had no idea it was there before this. Am I now guilty of a felony?

ANSWER: No. Only if the display is rude, careless, angry, or threatening — and done in the presence of another person. Still, you can now see why this is such a bad law. If you were adjusting the spray bottle, and someone saw you -- and told a police officer -- would he think this was "careless"? If he did, you could be arrested for a felony! You'd probably win your case -- but who would want to be in that kind of predicament? This is a really dangerous law, and I suggest you write your state legislators to remove it.

QUESTION: I am a teacher. I have always kept my firearm locked in my car so I have it available when I leave. I drive through some dangerous areas. Can this now be forbidden?

116

ANSWER: Yes.   If the school district (not the principal) actually passes, adopts, and publishes a written policy forbidding you to park on school property — you commit a felony by doing so, so long as you did so "knowingly and willfully".

QUESTION: What if my wife drops me off in the school parking lot, and such a published policy exists? Can we still have a firearm or weapon in the car securely encased or not readily accessible?

ANSWER: No problem. The school district may not restrict anything but actual parking privileges in the sense of leaving a vehicle unattended.

QUESTION: What about the federal restrictions? Doesn't this forbid mere possession within 1000 feet of any school zone?

ANSWER: Very perceptive question. The answer, assuming the law is constitutional, is "yes".   Only a concealed permit holder, school security guard, or police officer is going to be able to get within 1000 feet of an elementary or secondary school. However, since only a federal officer is going to make an arrest for this — I wouldn't worry too much unless you are dealing drugs, robbing a bank, or blowing something up.

QUESTION: I take my child to his bus stop. This is not a great section of town.   I carry pepper spray for protection. What can I do to protect myself?

ANSWER: Get a concealed permit. Then you would be fine, although you would have to carry it concealed. Otherwise, stay at least "one foot" away from the school bus stop — assuming you can figure out the boundaries of it. Also, write your legislator to revise the statute so that it only pertains to unmarried persons under 21 years of age. That would also take care of the problem the legislature was trying to cure.

TRAINING CHILDREN TO BE SAFE:

Most accidents happen due to either ignorance, carelessness, or a combination of both factors. The way to counter these dangers is to train children what to do when they see a firearm. The approved method by the NRA is to teach a child who sees a firearm to do the following:

a.   Don't touch the firearm.
b.   Leave the area.
c.   Immediately tell an adult

This is a great rule, and should also apply to ammunition, and to any toy guns that look real. I don't like the idea of a toy gun that looks real being anywhere near my house -- because the guns I own are real -- and some of the smaller calibers, especially a derringer, look like a toy! I don't want my kid to think it's O.K. to play with something that might be a gun, or could be confused with a toy. Guns are for adults who have been trained in their handling, and for responsible "young adults" who have adult supervision, and training. Guns are dangerous. Only training prevents accidents. Think about it. Maybe you'll stop a disaster!

[This page is reserved for future use]

[This page is reserved for future use]

CHAPTER NINE

WHAT DEALERS SHOULD KNOW

I'm sure there are lots of things that licensed firearms dealers, and other weapons dealers should know. I'm also sure they probably know most of them by heart. But just in case, I thought it might be a good idea to cover some of the questions that dealers, and would-be dealers seem to ask me over and over. On top of that I want to cover those areas which pose potential problems. As a general rule this chapter is devoted primarily to licensed firearms dealers, rather than collectors, manufacturers, and importers -- but I'll make some exceptions from time to time. Plus, I guarantee that some of the answers will prove very interesting to everyone.

WHO MUST SECURE A FEDERAL LICENSE:

Any person or business entity (corporation or partnership) that has as its principal objective, from the sale or transfer of firearms, the goal of livelihood and profit -- needs to be federally licensed. The main question in defining this profit motive is predominantly one of obtaining pecuniary gain and livelihood, as opposed to other interests such as improving or liquidating a personal collection. If all you're doing is making an occasional sale to thin your collection, or make room for some other purchases, or even to liquidate your entire collection, you don't need a federal license. If it's as a business -- you better have an FFL, or you are in deep buffalo chips.

WHAT DOES THE LICENSE COVER:

Well, in a nutshell, it allows you to purchase and ship firearms and ammunition to and fro any other FFL, no matter where they are located -- and otherwise engage in the business of buying and selling firearms, as a business. It also allows you to loan firearms for temporary lawful sporting purposes.

It does not cover personal carrying -- that is determined by the law of the state you are in. In Florida, this is covered by F.S. 790.25(3)(i), which permits a dealer, or employee, to carry while engaged in the "lawful course of such business." So, if you think you can carry just because you have the FFL -- think again.

LICENSED COLLECTORS:

The only reason anyone would want to be a licensed collector is if you want to buy, sell, and transport curios and relics, out of your residence state. Other than as to curios and relics -- you are treated exactly as a non-licensee.

A relic is a firearm manufactured at least 50 years previous, and it cannot be a replica, but must be the real thing. A curio must be certified as curio due to it being novel, rare, bizarre, or connected to a historical event. Before it becomes a "curio", a specified procedure must be followed.

OBTAINING THE FFL:

If you want to become a dealer, assuming you are 21 years of age, and otherwise qualify, you can get the application from your local office of the Bureau of Alcohol, Tobacco, and Firearms -- referred to as either the "ATF" or "BATF". Before your application will be accepted you should have a "place of business" to operate as an FFL (ie: Federal Firearms Licensee). The location must be a permitted use under state and local law -- which means that if you're zoned only for residential -- you better find another location if you want a license. Since your home is probably not zoned for firearms sale or storage -- it is doubtful it would qualify. Moreover, the portion of the premises used for your business must be "open to the public" -- and I doubt you want people walking in and out of your home during regular business hours, or have ATF agents nosing around while administrative and records searches are conducted there. Last, do not use a "cover" address for your license, and then work from your home, as your license wouldn't cover it. U.S. v. Bailey, 123 F.3d 1381 (11CCA 1997).

DENIAL OF APPLICATION:

Once you apply, your application will be approved or denied within sixty (60) days of submission, unless the application was deficient. If so, you'll be given thirty (**30**) days to correct it, and send it back. On those rare occasions where no approval or denial is obtained within the 60 day review period -- there is a way to force a decision under federal statute 28 USC 1361. This procedure will not be discussed in this book. Assuming your application is denied, the ATF Regional Director will issue you a Form 4498 denial, and you will then have fifteen (**15**) days to request a hearing to review the denial. If you don't request the hearing your application is disapproved, so marked, and returned to you. All notices are sent certified mail, return receipt requested -- and you should do likewise, although you are not under that same obligation.

The Regional Director must then give you at least ten (**10**) days written notice of the hearing date, and it must be held at a location convenient to you -- generally at the nearest regional office vs. Washington, D.C. If the denial stands -- a certified copy of the findings and conclusions are furnished to you on a Form 4501, which is marked as "disapproved".

If you're not real pleased with the result, you can still go another step. You then have sixty (**60**) days to file a petition for review with the United States District Court in your area, pursuant to the federal statute, 18 USC 923(f)(3), for a de novo judicial review of the denial.

PROCEDURE ON REVOCATION OF FFL:

If the Regional Director has reason to believe that you, or an employee, have willfully violated the requirements of the Gun Control Act of 1968, and any of the regulations you must operate by, he may revoke your license by mailing the licensee by certified mail, return receipt requested, a notice of revocation on a Form 4500. This factually states the violations.

At that point, you have fifteen (**15**) days to request a hearing to review the revocation, otherwise the Regional Director will issue a final notice on Form 4501. If you do request a hearing, the Regional Director, in the interest of justice, may postpone the effective date of revocation, or authorize continued operations pending judicial review. The administrative hearing procedure, and judicial review are the same as followed when an application for the FFL is denied.

If you are unlucky enough to be indicted for a felony, or crime punishable by more than two years imprisonment, or have had a criminal information filed against you for such, you may continue to operate until any conviction becomes final. Even then, you may apply to the Secretary of the Treasury for relief from disabilities if it's established that you are not likely to act in manner dangerous to public safety, and that such relief would not be contrary to the public interest.

If you are convicted of the felony, you may still file for removal of disability to operate as an FFL due to said conviction. If so, you are allowed to operate for thirty (**30**) days after the date of which conviction becomes final. If you don't file for this relief you must stop operating once the **30 days** after the date of the conviction runs.

If you were acquitted of the felony charges, or they are otherwise terminated by dismissal, ATF may not try to revoke your FFL for same reasons.

ADMINISTRATIVE REVIEW OF RECORDS AND INVENTORY:

Any licensee is subject to administrative audit of your books, records, and inventory. Unless it is pursuant to a search warrant, it will be done during normal business hours. You have no right to interfere, and should keep out of the agents way. If you think something is improper, mentally note it for review with your attorney at a later date. Do not play "big shot". It will only cause you trouble. Here is the way it works:

ATF may have a judicial magistrate issue a warrant upon "reasonable cause" to believe violation of the firearms law has occurred, and that evidence of such may be on business premises or other storage area. The warrant allows inspection of all records required to be kept, and all firearms & ammo kept on premises.

ATF agents may also inspect without reasonable cause, and without a warrant where:

1.   Such is done in the course of reasonable inquiry during a criminal investigation of someone other than the FFL.

2.   To ensure compliance with record keeping requirements, but not more than once in any 12 month period. However, the licensee may elect to conduct this inquiry at the local ATF office, rather than on the business premises.

3.   To determine the disposition of one or more particular firearms in course of bona fide criminal investigation.

If any records are seized, the BATF officer may seize only those records that constitute evidence of a violation, and copies must be provided within a reasonable time to licensee.

SALE OF FIREARMS/AMMUNITION TO LEGAL ALIENS:

Although somewhat confusing, it is legal for a firearms dealer to sell a firearm or ammunition to a resident alien. The alien must have been a legal resident in the state of sale for a "continuous" ninety (90) days, and be otherwise qualified. If the alien was a resident of Florida for a month or two, and moved somewhere else, and then back, start counting anew. The alien must be there continuously for an entire 90 day period to establish residency. Aliens who have a non-immigration visa are now normally prohibited from purchasing firearms due to the passage of the Omnibus Appropriations Act of 1999. This excludes from purchase students, and most temporary visitors. There is a rather complicated waiver procedure. There are also exceptions for aliens specifically admitted into in the country for hunting or sporting purposes, foreign law enforcement officers here on official business, and official representatives of friendly foreign governments. I would check with ATF before doing a sale to one of these exempted classes.

Assuming the alien is going to take the firearm out of the country, he needs a DSP Form 5 from the Office of Munitions Control in the State Department. Good luck.

BRADY LAW REQUIREMENTS:

Since Florida has an instantaneous record check procedure, we do not have a federal waiting period. However, the Florida Constitution requires a three (3) day waiting period on sales of all handguns unless the purchaser is the holder of a valid Florida concealed weapons permit, or the purchase is a trade for another handgun. Where the purchaser is a concealed permit holder, you need to photostat his permit, and attach it to the Form 4473. The Florida Constitution was changed in 1998, and a county may now pass by ordinance up to a five day waiting period on sales of any firearm to non-permit holders on public property -- ie: gun shows. This will vary county-to-county. Concealed Permit holders are not affected.

SALES OR DISPOSITIONS FROM PERSONAL COLLECTION:

As long as the firearm has been in your personal collection for at least one year from receipt, you may dispose of it as a personal firearm. However, the disposition must still be logged in your bound volume. You should have noted its receipt into your personal collection the same way.

SALE OF MULTIPLE FIREARMS TO SINGLE INDIVIDUAL:

If you sell two or more handguns of any type to the same individual within five (5) consecutive business days, you must report it on a Form 3310.4 -- not later than close of business date of each such transaction. In other words, if the non-licensee buys two handguns on Monday -- you must file on Monday. If he buys another on Thursday, you must file another one, because it's now "three handguns" within five business days. The Brady Bill also requires reporting it to the state, or local law enforcement.

THEFT OF FIREARMS:

If any firearm is stolen or lost from your inventory or collection, it must be reported to ATF, and to local police within 48 hours. This is primarily because Brady has made theft of firearms from a federal licensee, a federal offense.

PAWNBROKERS:

Pawnbrokers who buy, sell, transfer, or hold firearms as security for a loan must be federally licensed. While filling out the Form 4473 is not needed when the firearm is pledged for security, the receipt of such must still be entered into your bound volume. However, the Form 4473 must be completed when the firearm is redeemed -- as that is considered a "disposition" of the firearm. The NICS check must also be done.

On the other hand, if the disposition is to the same person who pledged the firearms with you, and more than one firearm is involved -- it need not be reported as a multiple sale on the Form 3310.4.

Even if the person who pledged the firearm is the same person seeking to redeem it -- it cannot be returned to an underaged person, or any other disqualified person, and should only be returned to person who pawned the firearm, or the ticketholder. If it's a handgun, you could not legally return it to an out-of-state resident, even if he was a Florida resident at the time of the pawn. Nor could you return it to him if he was under 21 years of age -- even if he was the person who legally pawned it.

SELLING TO PERSONS WITH OBVIOUS IMPAIRMENTS:

Not to long ago K-Mart was ordered to pay $12.5 million dollars for selling a rifle to an intoxicated person, who then went out, and shot someone. Technically, this sale violated no law, although it came awful close. The problem was that the jury felt it was negligent to sell a firearm to an obviously intoxicated person, and most juries would probably agree. [135] This should warn you that if you sell to someone who appears mentally imbalanced, appears to be using illegal drugs (even marijuana), or appears to have had too much to drink -- don't make the sale unless you have a spare twelve-and-a-half million!

Florida law doesn't allow an intoxicated person to use a loaded firearm except in necessary self-defense. That means there's a loophole if it's unloaded. The loophole applies only to the criminal violation -- negligence and recklessness are still civilly actionable, and that's where the money is -- or will go. In sustaining that 12.5 million verdict, here's what the Florida Supreme Court said:

> "One who knowingly sells an article to a person incompetent in its use, with reasonable foreseeability that injury to others may occur as a result of such use, can be held accountable in tort to others for the injuries sustained thereby."

If the guy gets drunk, or shoots cocaine after he buys the firearm, you should be off the legal hook -- unless you knew, or reasonably should have known that he was an alcoholic, incompetent, illegal drug user, or was planning to do something criminal. If you do -- you're in for lots of problems. So, be forewarned.

SELLING TO KIDS:

I know, we've been over this several times. It's easy when you talk about firearms -- 21 for a handgun -- 18 for a longgun. But, what about other weapons?

Well, if the kid is 18 years old he can buy anything he wants from a dealer except a handgun, and illegal weapons. No permission needed.

If the kid is under 18 years of age -- you can't sell anything but a common pocketknife without the permission of mom or dad, and the sale (money exchange), and delivery should be with the parent, not with the kid. Don't be cute, and hand junior the purchase Dad just bought for him -- give it to Dad, and let him hand it to junior. If you don't take my warning, and you deliver a firearm, bowie knife, dirk, brass knuckles, or electronic weapon -- it's a second degree felony. [136] Any other weapon is a third degree felony. An airgun may be considered a weapon. Generally, that depends on its use, or intended use. I would say a bow and arrow is always a weapon, because that's what it was traditionally used for. But, why take the chance? Just sell the darn thing direct to Dad, and skip all the possible legal hassles.

Another quirk is that although you can sell a person under 21 years, but at least 18 years of age a shotgun or rifle — a shotgun with a pistol grip in lieu of a shoulder stock does not qualify as a "shotgun" because a shotgun, pursuant to 18 USC 921(a)(5) is a weapon "intended to be fired from the shoulder." When the shoulder stock is missing, it is no longer intended to be "fired from the shoulder", hence — it's not a shotgun. The legal way around this is to sell the gun with a shoulder stock. If done that way, even if the stock is not attached — the sale is legal. See, FFL Newsletter, February 1999, page 3. 27 CFR 178.99(b).

SALE OF AMMUNITION TO MINOR:

Florida law does not make it a crime for a non-federal licensee to sell ammunition to a minor. A federal licensee could not. However, the loophole has been somewhat covered in the 1994 Crime Bill by making it illegal for <u>anyone</u> to sell or transfer handgun ammunition to a juvenile under the age of 18 years, except under very precise exceptions. Thus, a federal licensee can't sell handgun ammunition to anyone under 21 years of age, and a private citizen can't sell it to anyone under 18 years of age.

As I already pointed out in a footnote, Wal-Mart got socked with a substantial civil jury verdict for causing the death of an individual because they sold handgun ammunition to an under-aged youth who then used it to shoot the decedent. The appellate court held that this was exactly the conduct that the federal statute tried to prevent, thus a violation of the statute was negligence, and the cause of the misfortune.

A warning to the wise is sufficient!

REQUIRED WARNING NOTICES UPON SALE:

It is a second degree misdemeanor for any retailer to fail to provide the following written warning in letters no less than 1/4 inch in height to the transferee when you sell or deliver a firearm.

IT IS UNLAWFUL, AND PUNISHABLE BY IMPRISONMENT AND FINE, FOR ANY ADULT TO STORE OR LEAVE A FIREARM IN ANY PLACE WITHIN THE REACH OR EASY ACCESS OF A MINOR UNDER 18 YEARS OF AGE OR TO KNOWINGLY SELL OR OTHERWISE TRANSFER OWNERSHIP OR POSSESSION OF A FIREARM TO A MINOR OR A PERSON OF UNSOUND MIND.

A similar warning must be posted at each purchase counter (including gun shows) in block letters at least 1" inch in height. This written warning must be given to the purchaser, even if he is 70 years old, has no kids, doesn't know any kids, and has no desire to. It must be in block letters at least one quarter inch high. If you think this is no big deal -- remember the verdict in K-Mart. What do you think a jury will do if some kid gets hold of the firearm, and the jerk who bought it from you says he didn't know he had to keep it in a safe place away from the child? I bet you can guess!

IT IS UNLAWFUL TO STORE OR LEAVE A FIREARM IN ANY PLACE WITHIN THE REACH OR EASY ACCESS OF A MINOR UNDER 18 YEARS OF AGE OR TO KNOWINGLY SELL OR OTHERWISE TRANSFER OWNERSHIP OR POSSESSION OF A FIREARM TO A MINOR OR PERSON OF UNSOUND MIND.

This means at gun shows, and at your place of business. True, it's only a second degree misdemeanor. But then, there's that silly verdict in K-Mart popping-up again. Get the point?

Federal law also requires a posted notice both on the licensed premises, and at gun shows regarding the requirements of the Youth Safety Handgun Act. These posters are available through ATF, and repeat the restrictions set forth on ATF Form I 5300.2. You may order this through the ATF Distribution Center at (703) 455-7801.

STUFF YOU GOTTA SELL:

The Omnibus Appropriations Act of 1999 requires that all FFL's now sell, and have in stock secure gun storage devices. This means trigger locks, gun locking devices which render the firearm unable to discharge, lock boxes with locks, or gun safes. You can lose your license for not having these in stock unless they are on reorder, or the manufacturer is temporarily out.

STUFF YOU JUST CAN'T SELL IN FLORIDA:

It's illegal to manufacture, sell, or try to sell any weapon commonly known as brass knuckles, or a slungshot to anyone, even an adult. Under F.S. 790.09, this would be a second degree misdemeanor. On the other hand, it's not illegal to own them. Now, you know what brass knuckles are (calling them a "paper weight" is bull) , but a "slung-shot" or "slapshot" -- is a weighted material fixed on the end of a flexible handle or strap, to be used as a weapon. While a telescoping "tactical baton" may act in a similar fashion, it's not the same animal, and in my opinion is perfectly legal.

Another problem is "hoax bombs". Under federal law a dummy shell or grenade is not a destructive device or weapon -- it's just a dummy grenade. They make great paper weights! Many of my friends have one. The problem is that under Florida law -- they appear to be illegal due to some really crummy drafting of a statute, Florida Statute 790.165. If you want to be on the safe side, as silly as it may sound, you should not sell, transfer, or possess these little gems.

Since I'm sure you'd like to know what a "hoax bomb" is -- it's any device or object that by its design, construction, content, or characteristics appears to be a destructive device, or appears or is represented to contain an explosive. So much for "dummy dynamite" clocks in those nifty gag catalogs! People just can't have any fun with these stupid laws!

Anyway, the real bad news is that it's a third degree felony to make these things, sell them, possess them, or deliver them unless you're a member of a theatrical company utilizing them as a prop -- or if you're a security person in an airport using them within your duties as you try to sneak them past detectors to see if anyone notices. Of course, we all know that this law makes no sense, as written. On the other hand, I think the statute would have a hard time withstanding a constitutional attack, unless the "hoax bomb" was being used with criminal intent. Test case time, again.

SELF-PROPELLED, BALLISTIC, OR "SPRING" KNIVES:

Lastly, you can't own, sell, possess, or transfer a self-propelled, ballistic, or "spring knife". Violation is a first degree misdemeanor.[137] A self-propelled, or ballastic knife, or "spring knife", is a device that propels a knifelike blade as a projectile by means of a coiled spring, elastic, or compressed gas. They used to make them as belt buckles. In Florida, it's a no no. In Federal land — it's a ten year felony. 15 USC 1245

GUN SHOWS:

Gun shows have come under great criticism, primarily by people who don't want you to own guns. For the most part, the criticism is totally unwarranted. However, there is one thing about gun shows that poses a serious problem -- and that's non-FFL's having tables where they sell firearms out of their "private" collections. These "private" sales are often being conducted as a regular weekend business by persons who are not following the law, and are hurting the industry as a whole by doing so. ATF has already sent warnings to some of these people, and has cracked down on others. I have handled some of these cases. I think you should think seriously about it if you are a non-FFL, and are basically conducting a weekend business in firearms. BATF is watching!

The same thing applies to reloaders who do not have an FFL. Since they are reloading as a business, they are "manufacturers", and need to be federally licensed under 18 USC 923.

FIREARM INSTRUCTORS:

Firearm instructors who certify students for concealed weapons permits, as of July 1998, must now maintain records which certify that he or she observed the student safely handle and discharge the firearm. HB 3713 (1998). F.S. 790.06(2)(h). This may be a simple list of the students names, and date observed. You keep the records for two (2) years..

You should also remember that any certificate you send up to Tallahassee should have your NRA i/d number, or K license number.

FFL OPERATING OUT OF HOME:

This is a quick-update section for FFL's whose business address is different from where they keep their inventory, records, ship from, etc. A definite federal no-no. Such was the case in U.S.v. Bailey, 123 F.3 1381 (11CCA 1997), where Mr. Bailey got convicted of the federal offense of "dealing without a license" because the license covers only specified business premises, and Mr. Bailey was actually working out of his home. Be warned! Serious stuff!

CHAPTER TEN
THE ASSAULT WEAPONS BAN

BACKGROUND ON THE ASSAULT WEAPONS BAN:

In 1994 the Congress bowed to media pressure, and sold out the free American public by passing certain portions of the Crime Bill, which are now law. The primary portion of the Bill now appears in 18 USC 922 (v) & (w). A reflection of the Bill makes it clear that most politicians are interested in appropriations, and re-elections -- not the rights of the People. In case you don't already know, these firearms are not the problem the media and most anti-gun advocates would like you to believe, even the FBI admits that in its statistics. With the exception of MAC and TEC-type weapons, most are too large to be easily concealed, and because of this the handgun is still the weapon of choice of criminals.

Of course, the handgun is also the weapon of choice of most honest citizens who are trying to defend themselves from criminals.[138]

From a historic point of view, the "assault weapon" is probably the weapon that the Second Amendment would protect the most -- because it is the only firearm available to the general public that could stand a fighting chance against government troops. And, if you didn't read Chapter One, that was one of the key points of the Second Amendment -- to have an armed citizenry that could overthrow a tyrannical government, if it ever came to that point. I don't think it ever will -- and I certainly wouldn't ever want to see that happen. There are no good wars -- and civil wars are the absolute worst. Look at Bosnia, or Lebanon. Both beautiful countries that are now hell holes. The Oklahoma City bombing is another good example of why this type of thinking belongs in the Twilight Zone.

On the other hand, I don't want to be caught without a means of defending myself, either. A concentration camp is not my idea of a good place to live. Moreover, this type of firearm is a heck of a good gun to have if there's a riot, and a few dozen screaming fruitcakes have decided that your home or business would be swell to loot, and would look real good going up in flames.

Anyway, let's hope it never comes to that, but we've all seen that the police and National Guard aren't gonna be of much help to you if it does. Basically, you'll be on your own, and when that happens -- I want a gun I can count on.

Sorry, President Clinton -- that's just the way it is! You've got your bodyguards -- I've just got me.

Oh, well. You now know something of my warped philosophy of life -- or, at least something about my concerns. However, since this book is about the law -- here's some of the new bad news with the passage of the Assault Weapons Ban in the 1994 Crime Bill.

GENERAL PROVISIONS OF THE BAN:

With passage of the Crime Bill, it's now a federal crime to manufacture, transfer, sell, or possess any semiautomatic assault weapon manufactured or imported **after the effective date** of the Act. If you've got one manufactured or imported before -- you're OK. This includes any type of ammunition drum, feed strip, or magazine that is capable of holding more than ten (10) rounds, whether such device is for an assault weapon, or not -- if the weapon, or the magazine was not lawfully possessed on the date the law is enacted. A magazine, feed strip, or drum that is capable of accepting in excess of ten rounds is defined as a "large capacity ammunition feeding device". Yes, that includes the clip for your pistol — assuming it was manufactured after the effective date, September 13, 1994.

To make it somewhat easier for you to determine when the firearm or magazine was manufactured, the law requires that all such firearms or magazines manufactured after the date of the law's enactment, have the date of manufacture clearly included in their serial number. However, since these things are being manufactured only for the police or military after the effective date — they shouldn't be on the market unless something very illegal happened. In other words — don't be too concerned if you buy it through a dealer — their stock should be fine, even if it exceeds the ten rounds. Lots and lots of these magazines were manufactured or imported just before the ban so that they would be in inventory.

EXEMPTED FIREARMS:

The law, as written, exempts any firearm that is manually operated by a bolt, pump, lever, or slide action. It also exempted antique firearms, firearms rendered permanently inoperable, any semi-automatic that <u>cannot accept</u> a detachable magazine holding more than five rounds of ammunition at a time, and a whole list of firearms which were exempted for no reason in particular, other than it would have ticked-off too many people if Congress included them, and banned future manufacture. Other than that, the definitions of what firearms technically fall within the new definition of "assault weapons" appear after the upcoming chart:

CHART OF EXEMPTED TYPES OF FIREARMS:

Firearms exempted from the ban			
bolt action	pump action	lever action	slide action
antique firearm	semi-auto w max 5 round capacity	prior to 9/13/94 or exempted	permanently inoperable (welded)

SEMI-AUTOMATIC ASSAULT WEAPON:

A "<u>semi-automatic assault weapon</u>" under the present law includes any of the following firearms, copies, or duplicates, manufactured or imported after the ban, known as:

A.   Norinco, Mitchell, and Poly Tech AK's (Avtomat Kalashnikov -- all models)
B.   Action Arms Israeli Military Industries Uzi, and Galil
C.   Beretta Ar-70 (SC-70)
D.   Colt AR-15
E.   Fabrique National FN/FAL, FN/LAR, FNC
F.   SWD M-10, M-11, M-11/9, M-12
G.   Steyr AUG
H.   Intratec TEC-9, TEC-DC9, TEC22
I.   Any revolving cylinder shotgun such as the Street Sweeper and Striker 12.

UNNAMED SEMI-AUTOMATIC RIFLES:

Also banned in the law are semi-automatic rifles imported or manufactured after the ban that have the ability to accept[139] a detachable magazine, and have two (2) or more of the following characteristics:

a. A folding or telescopic stock.
b. A pistol grip that protrudes conspicuously beneath the action.
c. A bayonet mount.
d. A flash suppressor, or threaded barrel that can accommodate one.
e. A grenade launcher.

UNNAMED SEMI-AUTOMATIC PISTOLS:

Also banned in the law are semi-automatic pistols manufactured or imported after the ban that have the ability to accept a detachable magazine (ie: everything but a revolver), and have two (2) or more of the following characteristics:

a. A magazine that attaches outside of the pistol grip
b. A threaded barrel.
c. A shroud that is attached to, or partially or completely encircles the barrel which permits the shooter to hold the firearm with the non-trigger hand, without being burned.
d. Has a manufactured weight of 50 ounces or more when unloaded.

UNNAMED SEMI-AUTOMATIC SHOTGUNS:

Also banned in the law are semi-automatic shotguns manufactured or imported after the ban that have two (2) or more of the following:

a. A folding or telescopic sight
b. A pistol grip that protrudes conspicuously beneath the action.

c.   A fixed ammunition capacity in excess of five (5) rounds.

d.   Has the ability to accept any detachable magazine.

TRANSFER OF AN ASSAULT WEAPON, OR LARGE CAPACITY FEEDING DEVICE:

Under the present law, if you obtain a pre-ban assault weapon, or large capacity feeding device -- you have no paperwork required on a private, non-dealer transfer or resale. However, it might be smart to hang on to any receipt -- although it's not required.

EXEMPTED FIREARMS:

The drafters of the Bill included a listing of over 650 firearms, including replicas and duplicates from other manufacturers, that were gratuitously "excepted" from the Bill, including both past and future manufacture. Thus, the firearms on this "Schedule A" exemption list can still be manufactured and sold. In actuality, most of the named firearms did not fit the statutory definition of an "assault weapon", anyway -- since they are manually operated by a lever, bolt, pump, or slide action -- or are not capable of holding five rounds of ammunition. In other words, the sponsors tried to downplay the effect of the Bill by publicizing a supposedly large number of "exempted" weapons, that really had nothing to do with the proposed law in the first place. Neat, huh?

With this exciting knowledge, let me give you the partial list of those firearms which are definitely exempted, and which might otherwise have fallen within the definition of an assault weapon:

Centerfire Autoloading Rifles:

Browning: BAR Mark II Safari semi-auto rifle, & Safari Magnum rifle; High-Power rifle. Heckler & Koch: Model 300 rifle. Iver Johnson: M-1, & 50th Anniversary M-1. Marlin: Model 9 camp carbine; model 45 carbine. Remington: Nylon 66 auto loading rifle; Model 7400 rifle, model 7400 auto rifle, & model 7400 special purpose auto rifle. Ruger: Mini-14 autoloading (w/o folding stock); Mini-Thirty rifle.

Rimfire Autoloading Rifles:

AMT: Lightning 25/22 rifle; Lightning small game hunting rifle II; Magnum Hunter auto rifle; Anschutz: 525 deluxe auto. Armscor: model 20P auto rifle. Browning: Auto-22 rifle & Auto 22 Grade VI. Krico: model 260 auto rifle. Lakefield Arms: model 64B auto rifle. Marlin models: 60 self loading rifle; 60ss self loading; 70HC auto; 9901 self loading rifle; 70P Papoose; 922 Magnum self loading rifle; 995 self loading rifle. Norinco: Model 22 ATD rifle. Remington: Model 522 Viper autoloading rifle; 552BDL Speedmaster rifle. Ruger: 10/22 autoloading carbine (w/o folding stock). Survival Arms: AR-7 Explorer rifle. Texas Remington: revolving carbine. Voere: Model 2115 auto rifle.

Competition Rifles -- Center & Rimfire

Anschutz: 64-MS Left Silhouette; 1808D RT Super Match 54 Target; 1827B Biathlon rifle; 1903D match rifle; 1803D Intermediate match; 1911 match rifle; 54.18MS REP Delux Silhouette rifle; 1913 super match rifle; 1907 match rifle; 1910 super match II; 54.18MS Silhouette rifle; Super Match 54 Target model 2013; Super Match 54 Target model 2007. Beeman/Feinwerkbau: 2600 target rifle. Cooper Arms: Model TRP-1 ISU standard rifle. E.A.A.: Weihrauch HW 60 target rifle; HW 660 Match rifle. Finnish Lion: Standard Target Rifle. Krico models: 360 S2 Biathlon rifle; 400 Match Rifle; 360S Biathlon rifle; 500 Kricotronic Match rifle; 600 Sniper rifle; 600 Match rifle. Lakefield Arms models: 90B Target rifle; 91T Target rifle; 92S Silhouette rifle. Marlin model 2000 target rifle. Mauser: Model 86-SR Specialty rifle. McMillan: M-86 Sniper rifle; Combo M-87/ M-88 50 caliber rifle; 300 Phoenix Long Range rifle; M-89 Sniper rifle; National Match rifle; Long Range rifle. Parker-Hale: M-87 Target rifle; M-85 Sniper rifle. Remington: 40-XB Rangemaster Target Centerfire; 40-XR KS Rimfire Position rifle; 40-XBBR KS; 40-XC KS National Match Course rifle. Sako: TRG-21 bolt action rifle. Steyr-Mannlicher: Match SPG-UIT rifle; SSG P-I rifle; SSG P-III rifle; SSG P-IV rifle. Tanner: Standard UIT rifle; 50 Meter Free rifle; 300 Meter Free rifle. Wichita: Silhouette rifle.

Autoloading Shotguns:

American Arms: Franchi Black Magic 48/AL. Benelli: Super Black Eagle shotgun; Super Black Eagle Slug gun; M1 Super 90 Field auto shotgun;

Montefeltro Super 90 shotgun; Montefeltro Super 90 20 gauge shotgun; M1 Sporting Special auto shotgun; Black Eagle Competition auto shotgun. Beretta: A-303 auto shotgun; 390 Field auto shotgun; 390 Super Trap & Super Skeet shotguns; Vittoria auto shotgun; Model 1201F auto shotgun. Browning: BSA 10 AUTO SHOTGUN; BSA Stalker auto shotgun; A-500R auto shotgun; A-500G auto shotgun; A-500G Sporting Clays; Auto-5 Light 12 & 20; Auto-5 Stalker; Auto-5 Magnum 20; Auto-5 Magnum 12. Churchill: Turkey automatic shotgun. Cosmi: automatic shotgun. Maverick: Model 60. Mossberg models: 5500; 9200 Regal semi-auto; 9200 USST auto shotgun; 9200 Camo Shotgun; 6000 auto shotgun. Remington: model 1100; 11-87 Premier shotgun; 11-87 Sporting Clays; 11-87 Premier Skeet; 11-87 Premier Trap; 11-87 Special Purpose Magnum; 11-87 SPS-T Camo auto shotgun; 11-87 Special purpose Deer gun; 11-87 SPS-BG-Camo Deer/Turkey shotgun; 11-87 SPS Deer shotgun; 11-87 Special Purpose Synthetic Camo; SP-10 Magnum Camo auto shotgun; SP-10 Magnum auto shotgun; SP-10 Magnum Turkey combo; 1100 LT-20 auto; 1100 Special Field; 1100 20 gauge Deer gun; 1100 LT-20 Tournament Skeet. Winchseter: model 1400 semi-auto shotgun.

THE AFTERMATH, AND SOME ANALYSIS:

Now, remember -- the assault weapons ban was supposedly a response to the large number of these weapons being used by gangs, et cetra, in the commission of crimes. However, the only thing the bill accomplished was to fuel a buying frenzy for these weapons, and cause a serious increase in their price. Thanks to the Bill, there are more of these weapons on the streets (and buried under them) than would have ever been possible without it. Whatever, the truth of the matter is that less than 1% of crimes committed with firearms involved so-called "assault" type weapons. Those are FBI statistics!

Now, if you thought that the Assault Weapons Bill was bad -- wait until you hear what else the Clinton Administration, Handgun Control, and Congress had planned for you. Senator Howard Metzenbaum of Ohio, and Representative Charles Schumer of New York introduced "Brady II" in Congress at the end of 1994, and have kept submitting it year after year.. If they can't get it through intact — they keep trying to get it in piecemeal. Currently, legislation is pending which would ban juveniles from firing an "assault weapon", even under adult supervision.   There was another one that would have made it illegal for five or more gun owners to meet together, armed.   (Hey! Didn't you know -- we're all gonna revolt — gotta protect Congress, somehow!)

All these new and recurrent bills are a gun owners nightmare, and would make the Second Amendment a sad joke, assuming it really still exists on anything but paper, anyway. In reality, the proposals pending are close reproductions of what Adolph Hitler passed in Germany back in 1935. They would require registration of all firearms (the prelude to an effective method to confiscate); banning of "Saturday Night Specials" (which is defined to include lots of handguns that you and I consider as great guns); making high velocity ammunition illegal (so we can just "wound" criminals and deer); banning all magazines which hold over six rounds; requiring a special "arsenal license" for households that have more than twenty firearms or 1000 rounds of ammunition, and allowing ATF inspections of all such homes without a warrant; limiting handgun purchases to one per month; classifying barrels, stocks, and actions as "firearms"; having a 50% tax on ammunition, etc. Other legislation slated for the agenda was lobbied by Handgun Control, Inc., which is funded by BlockBuster Video, and other corporate liberals.   There was even one that was going to make it a crime for an organization to inform its members (ie: the NRA & GOA) which of your representatives were anti-gun, etc.   That way — they could have gotten rid of both the Second Amendment, and the First Amendment in one swoop. Nice work, boys. So much for the First Amendment's guarantee of the Right of the People to Free Speech and Peacefully Assemble.

These people in Congress and the Senate are after you!   There is only one thing that really matters up on Capital Hill. (Yeah, I mis-spelled it) — getting re-elected!   Don't forget it!

A QUOTE FROM ADOLPH HITLER ON GUN CONTROL:

Just remember what Adolph Hitler said back in 1935:

"This year will go down in history. For the first time, a civilized nation has full gun registration. Our streets will be safer, our police more efficient, and the world will follow our lead into the future!"

A QUOTE FROM THOMAS JEFFERSON:

Compare that to what Thomas Jefferson once said, and you get a good perspective of where Second Amendment advocates are coming from:

> "Those who would sacrifice a little freedom for a little order, will lose both, and deserve neither."

MODIFICATIONS TO ASSAULT RIFLES:

Before you go modifying your SKS , or other assault type rifle, let me warn you that this is one confusing area of law! I have read this stuff over and over — and still had to call the Firearms Technology Branch of ATF to explain it to me. The law does not mean what it says unless you studied at "Alice In Wonderland University". Were it not for some letters from BATF published in the American Rifleman in 1994 in response to some questions from the NRA, and some great insight from the Firearms Technology Branch of ATF — I would never have included this section.[140]

To begin, you start with 18 USC 922 (r), which states:

> "It shall be unlawful for any person to <u>assemble</u> from <u>imported parts</u> any semiautomatic rifle or shotgun <u>prohibited from importation under section 925(d)(3)</u> of this chapter as not being particularly suitable for or readily adaptable to sporting purposes . . . ."

18 USC 925(d)(3) pertains to those firearms and types of ammunition which the Secretary of Treasury allows to be imported -- they are on a list which includes most SKS type firearms. Thus, subsection (d)(3) allows importation:

> " of a type that does not fall within the definition of a firearm as defined in section 5845(a) of the Internal Revenue Code of 1954 (ie: any NFA weapon), and is generally recognized as particularly suitable for or readily adaptable to sporting purposes . . . ."

In conjunction with all this, you need to know the federal regulation that implements the law, and deals with the modification or "assembly of semiautomatic rifles or shotguns", to wit: 27 CFR 178.39. The pertinent parts of that regulation read as follows:

(a)   No person shall assemble a semiautomatic rifle or any shotgun using more than 10 of the imported parts listed in paragraph (c) of this section if the assembled firearm is prohibited from importation under section 925(d)(3) as not being particularly suitable for or readily adaptable to sporting purposes.

(b)   The provisions of this section shall not apply to:

      (3)   The repair of any rifle or shotgun which had been imported into or assembled in the United States prior to November 30, 1990, or the replacement of any part of such firearm.

c.   For purposes of this section, the term imported parts are:

(1) Frames, receivers, receiver castings, forgings or stampings
(2) Barrels
(3) Barrel extensions
(4) Mounting blocks (trunions)
(5) Muzzle attachments
(6) Bolts
(7) Bolt carriers
(8) Operating rods
(9) Gas pistons
(10) Trigger housings
(11) Triggers
(12) Hammers
(13) Sears
(14) Disconnectors
(15) Buttstocks
(16) Pistol grips
(17) Forearms, handguards
(18) Magazine bodies
(19) Followers
(20) Floorplates

So, what the heck does all this mean? Well, you still need to read 58 Federal Register 40587 (July 29, 1993). That somewhat explains the application of 27 CFR 179 and 18 USC 922 (r). It states that it was to implement the Crime Control Act of 1990 by prohibiting the circumvention of the ban of nonsporting rifles and shotguns on domestically manufactured weapons thereby preventing the assembly of what are essentially foreign made firearms that would otherwise not be importable. So, if a rifle has more than half of the twenty essential parts listed in the regulation made from imported parts (ie: more than ten) — it is banned from assembly or further modification in the United States.

Now, remember — the unlawful part here is "assembly". To you, we mean "modification". Or, to put it another way — sale, possession, and purchase of these weapons, even if illegally modified, is not illegal! Only making of the modification is illegal!

However, there is one exception, and that applies both to imported, and domestic rifles and shotguns that meet the definitions in the 1994 assault weapons ban set forth in 18 USC 922(v). This is so because if you modify a firearm that is otherwise exempted in Schedule A, or was grandfathered in because it was a "pre-ban" weapon, and by that modification you now qualify the gun under the "two or more" banned parts in 18 USC 921(30)(B) — you have now "manufactured" a new firearm, and not only is the modification illegal — but sale, purchase, and possession are also illegal unless its for the government.

So, back to the question of what you can legally do to modify your SKS? Here's the safe list:

1. Replace the existing stock and handguard with a non-folding wooden or synthetic stock having either a Monte Carlo or thumbhole design.

2. Attach a muzzle-mounted recoil compensator that is <u>not</u> also designed as a flash suppressor.

3. Replace the fixed magazine with a detachable magazine — so long as you also replace the standard stock with a Monte Carlo or thumbhole design, and remove the bayonet mount completely from the firearm.

4. Replace the existing ten round fixed magazine with a five round fixed magazine, or install a block in the well of the ten round magazine limiting it to five rounds.

5. Replace the existing receiver cover with a cover having telescopic sight bases or rings.

6. Replace the front and/or rear sights.

7. Install an ambidextrous safety.

Adding a folding stock, bipod, flash hider, is not allowed, nor is adding a detachable magazine (unless you also have the Monte Carlo or thumbhole stock without a bayonet lug), because your federal government says that this renders it as "non-sporting", and thus would be banned from import pursuant to 18 USC 925(d)(3). Same thing about the bayonet on those imported after 1989, unless they are the Russian SKS on the curio and relic list.

QUESTION: Why can you have a bayonet mount on the Russian SKS?

ANSWER: Because it's on the curio and relic list issued by the Secretary of Treasury, and thus can be imported with the bayonet under 18 USC 925 (e)(1)

"Notwithstanding any other provision of this title, the Secretary shall authorize the importation of, by any licensed importer, the following: (1) All rifles and shotguns listed as curios or relics by the Secretary . . ." 18 USC 925(e)(1)

I hope this has been of some help to you. It is not the final word on modifications, and I didn't intend it to be. This is not my area of expertise, and I don't want to give you any bad advise. If you decide to modify your SKS, or anything else — good luck!

CHAPTER ELEVEN

SELF DEFENSE, AND THE LAWFUL USE OF FORCE

SOME PRACTICAL PROBLEMS OF SELF-DEFENSE:

Your rights to defense of self, family, and property all have different rules. Understanding the rules are important if you are a responsible individual. If not, understanding the rules are still important to avoid criminal prosecution, or civil liability.

One thing I must say at the beginning of this chapter is a word on the practicality of using self-defense. The criminal always has the advantage, because he is not afraid to use his weapon illegally. Moreover, you may fall into the trap of trying to decide if your use of the weapon is legal, or not. If you miss, or not. If you get sued, prosecuted, or not. All of these things, and more will be going through your mind, and all are unfortunately to your disadvantage from a standpoint of survival. However, they are the law, and must be followed to whatever extent you reasonably can.

When people ask me when they can use a firearm, I tell them that from a practical, and not necessarily legal standpoint -- the only time anyone should know you have a weapon, or ever see the weapon -- is when you're ready to use it, sure you can use it, and can legally pull the trigger.

Why?

For one thing, it gives you the advantage of surprise. This split second advantage is often the difference between who is lying dead on the ground -- you or him. If you chose not to fire the weapon, and hope that by displaying it the other person will desist in his felonious conduct (you can never use a deadly weapon to stop a misdemeanor) -- good luck. At least you still have a momentary advantage.

But whatever the situation -- as soon as the weapon is displayed, or you threaten to draw it, whether you are justified or not -- you have probably escalated the situation. There is no real way of turning back once it comes out. The situation tends to intensify, rather than get better -- unless the guy runs, or surrenders.

The real question then becomes whether the other person is willing to push his luck -- or whether you are willing to take another life to protect your own, to protect the life of your loved ones, or in certain instances, to protect your property. Don't think you can just wound him, or shoot the knife out of his hand. It doesn't work that way. Modern thinking in the instructional area of self-defense is to keep shooting until your opponent falls to the ground, incapacitated. Until that happens, he's still a very lethal threat, and one shot is rarely enough to stop an attack -- even if it's enough to kill him. An attacker who dies in a hospital three hours after you shoot him, still has two hours and fifty minutes to kill you, and your family before he dies. If you think I'm kidding you -- don't! It happens all too often. Ask any police officer.

Obviously, if you get into one of these predicaments, and misjudge the situation, you will either be dead, or be prosecuted. Neither alternative seems very fair, and it rarely is. However, these are some of the facts of real life, and let me assure you that no honest, responsible citizen wants to carry a weapon or firearm. Unfortunately, it's just come to that point if you want to survive. On the other hand, you must somehow manage to keep your cool, and act responsibly. Certainly, in this type of circumstance -- that will be a very difficult, if not an impossible task.

On this happy note we start the most important chapter in this book -- your current right to self-defense under Florida law. The first part of this is understanding some basic definitions which are essential to having the slightest idea of what your rights or liabilities are. Here goes:

FORCIBLE FELONY

Before you learn anything else, you need to know what a "forcible felony" is.[141] Knowing this is very important because it defines when you can use a deadly weapon in self-defense, and when you can't. Of course, a "deadly weapon" is one that is likely to cause death or great bodily harm.[142] Thus, the only time you can use a firearm, or any other deadly weapon in self-defense is when it is used to stop or prevent a "forcible felony."[143] And, by the way, "use" doesn't necessarily mean "firing" the weapon -- pointing it may also constitute use -- so be real careful. More about this when we discuss aggravated assault.

The list of forcible felonies in Florida is as follows:[144]

1.   Treason
2.   murder
3.   manslaughter
4.   sexual battery
5.   robbery, including carjacking & home invasions
6.   burglary
7.   arson
8.   kidnapping
9.   aggravated assault
10.   aggravated battery
11.   aircraft piracy
12.   unlawful throwing/placing or discharging of a bomb or destructive device
13.   aggravated stalkiing
14.   unlawful discharge/placing/throw destructive devices
15.   any other felony (not misdemeanor) which involves the use, or threat of physical force or violence against any person (not animals -- persons!)

Now, the list of forcible felonies may seem all very clear on paper, but I can assure you that it's not as simple as you may think. You still cannot just shoot someone for the heck of it, even if they are committing a forcible felony. Your use of deadly force must still be "reasonable". To help you along on this rather varying system of what is legal or not, we'll move on to the specific statutes that define the parameters of lawful self-defense, but before we do, I think you should also be aware of a few more important definitions:

DEADLY WEAPON:

A "deadly weapon" is one that is likely to produce death or great bodily harm depending on its designed use, or the way it is used.[145] A firearm is always a deadly weapon according to the law,[146] however, a baseball bat, or any other instrument capable of inflicting death, or great bodily harm can also be a deadly weapon -- depending on its use, or intended use.[147]   For instance, a stone could be a deadly weapon depending on size, and circumstances of its use. Same thing for an ice pick, or screwdriver. And certainly, a bow and arrow would be a deadly weapon, because it would then be an instrument that was designed to inflict death or great bodily harm. Obviously, it all depends.

IMMINENT:

The next important definition is a word used all the time in self-defense statutes, to wit: "imminent". What does it mean?

It means something that is about to happen on an immediate basis. Not an hour from now, not a month from now, but usually within seconds, and if not -- it is so immediate that there is no way to reasonably avoid it.

REASONABLE BELIEF ("reasonably believes"):

What you reasonably believe the facts to be, and/or what you need to do to protect yourself, family, or property -- means just that. It must be objectively and subjectively reasonable under the particular circumstances, as they "reasonably" appeared to you at the time. This is not an easy definition since the reasonableness of your actions will be judged by others, rather than yourself, at a point in time well after the event has transpired. This after-the-fact analysis needs a real good lawyer, and sympathetic jury to assure your legal survival. A sympathetic police officer, and prosecutor wouldn't hurt, either, although you have a better chance with the police than the prosecutor.

So remember, that while you may have a personal belief that your neighbor, Herb, is from the Andrometer Star System, and is preparing an invasion of earth -- it is doubtful that the rest of your neighbors, judges, lawyers, and juries will go along with this. Thus, when you read the words of wisdom enacted by your Legislature that have limited your once God-given right to self-defense, try to remember that you must act within the terms of normal reality -- rather than the reality you'd like things to be.

The classic real example of this was when some elderly woman heard noise outside her house during the daylight hours, and decided there was a criminal outside who was going to burglarize her house and attack her. When she heard the guy make some noise immediately outside her front door, she grabbed a shotgun and shot it through the door. It killed him dead. Unfortunately for both, it was her milkman, and all he was doing was leaving her some milk. Yeah, it was reasonable to her -- she was scared of everything that moved. Shows you what watching T.V. can do to you. However, it had nothing to do with objective reasonability -- and she was convicted of homicide.

Just about the same thing happened not too long ago in another state where that poor Japanese kid got shot during Halloween by an over-reactive homeowner. The homeowners fears were real. That's what happens when you watch the news everyday, and start to take it too seriously. You can really lose perspective.

The homeowner had a good jury, and great lawyer in that case, and got off. But he still stands to lose everything if he gets sued civilly. Mistakes happen, huh?

A great quote on this subject is found in a Florida appellate court case decided in 1958 named <u>Harris v. State</u>. It succinctly states the philosophy of today's court in easy to understand terms:

> "Men do not hold their lives at the mercy of unreasonable fears or excessive caution of others . . . ."

DEADLY FORCE:

Deadly force, like a deadly weapon, is force <u>likely</u> to cause death or great bodily harm.[148] It doesn't legally matter whether either of these result from your actions -- it is legally enough that such might have caused, and was likely to cause death or great bodily harm. Great bodily harm can be a permanent or incapacitating injury or scar, or any other injury of a serious nature. A nosebleed is not a serious injury. A broken arm is.

Use of a firearm, baseball bat, metal pipe, ax handle, knife, etc. --

all are <u>likely</u> to be classified to involve the use of deadly force. Display of these items, combined with the threat of imminent violence, may constitute the felony of aggravated assault, or at least the first degree misdemeanor of improper exhibition of a dangerous weapon, unless there is a <u>legal</u> justification. Legal justifications are not necessarily what you'd like them to be, or think them to be. That's one of the problems.

JUSTIFIABLE USE OF FORCE -- NON-DEADLY FORCE:

OK, we've been discussing some concepts that relate to the use of deadly force, but what about non-deadly force? Actually, this area will give you considerably more leeway in what you can or cannot do. The problem, as with any use of force, is that it can <u>escalate</u> whatever situation you're in. In other words, anytime you use force, the likelihood is that the other party will use equal or greater force against you. Sooner or later this may get way out of proportion to the incident. However, since all you really want to know about is the law, rather than my silly interruptive comments, here it is:

A person is justified in using force, <u>except</u> deadly force, against another person, when and to the extent he <u>reasonably believes</u> that such force is necessary to defend himself or another from the other person's <u>imminent</u> use of <u>unlawful</u> force. (sounds familiar, huh?) This will normally apply to misdemeanors, and non-violent felonies that fall short of "forcible felonies".

Examples? A trespasser who won't leave, a person attacks you with fists, someone who tries to steal something from you short of a robbery or burglary, a person who is committing a criminal mischief on your property, or blocks you from the use of your property, a person who is so disorderly as to be committing a breach of the peace in your presence

and who will not desist, a person you have lawfully arrested (very "iffy") who resists your lawful arrest. If the criminal conduct involves only a trespass to real property -- then you must be a person who has a right or duty to protect it. If you don't -- then go call the police because your legislature seems to have screwed-up this law, too. It used to be that anyone could protect the property of anyone else, but this may not be the law today. I guess that's just part of where being a good neighbor has gone to.

QUESTION: How about the use of mace, a stun gun, or a Taser. These are non-deadly force, right?

ANSWER: They are certainly non-deadly force, but could still be "excessive force" which we'll be discussing soon. If the crime about to be perpetrated upon you involves physical violence -- it's my opinion that you should have an absolute right to use a non-deadly weapon to prevent harm to yourself, rather than having to battle-it-out with your hands.[149] If it involves a trespass, or property damage, I personally still feel the same way, but believe it becomes more "iffy", only because excessive force is usually a question of fact. Therefore, my opinion is of little use if somebody else disagrees -- especially if they're a judge or jury.

QUESTION: Is there anything else other than mace, a Taser, or a stun gun, that is non-deadly force?

ANSWER: Well, most knives, and all firearms are out, as are nun-chuks. These will be considered deadly weapons in almost any circumstance. Anything else depends on how it's being used. I mean, a full swing with a baseball bat is the use of deadly force -- but using it as a pole, to push someone away should not be. Fists, and kicking are generally not the use of deadly force -- but under appropriate circumstances, it's possible. The flat part of a shovel, or the flat part of a machete might not be, but then again, it might be real hard convincing a jury on that. The machete would be a real tough sell -- because most people think of it as a weapon, rather than as a tool. Obviously, in the hands of someone skilled, it can be used in a non-deadly manner. But, I think I'd rather pass on that particular trial. Anyway, you've got the idea.

EXCESSIVE FORCE:

As usual, the use of non-deadly force, and even deadly force, is limited to that amount you <u>reasonably believe</u> is necessary to prevent or terminate the other persons criminal conduct, or to reasonably protect yourself from harm. If you exceed this imaginary "reasonable" amount, your excess of force becomes "unreasonable", and becomes a criminal act to the extent that it is unreasonable, even if the use of force is otherwise legal.

JUSTIFIABLE USE OF DEADLY FORCE:

So, the bastard deserves to get shot. At least that's the way you feel. The real question is: how will the police and State Attorney feel about this course of conduct? This is the <u>real</u> crux of the problem! The law basically states that deadly force shall be used <u>only</u> if you <u>reasonably believe</u> that such force is <u>necessary</u> to prevent the <u>imminent</u> commission of a <u>forcible felony,</u> or prevent <u>imminent</u> death or great bodily harm to yourself or another.[150] If you'd like to see how this really works in a court of law, here's part of the Standard Jury Instruction that's read in a self-defense case:

> "In deciding whether the defendant was justified in the use of force likely to cause death or great bodily harm, you must judge him by the circumstances by which he was surrounded at the time the force was used. The danger facing the defendant need not have been actual; however, to justify the use of force likely to cause death or great bodily harm, the appearance of danger must have been so real that a reasonably cautious and prudent person under the same circumstances would have believed that the danger could be avoided only through the use of that force. Based upon appearances, the defendant must have actually believed that the danger was real." SJI 3.04(d).

Get a good jury -- you win. Get a bad jury, and you've got real serious problems. And we are not just talking criminal law here, because people are getting sued all the time for the excessive use of force -- which, by the way, is <u>not</u> covered by your Homeowners Insurance Policy. (Gads! How did that ever happen? More on that later)

Moreover, if you are the initial aggressor, or if you are in the process of perpetrating a forcible felony -- you may not have any rights to use deadly physical force, at all, even in self-defense, since you are the initial wrongdoer. Also, if you were not the initial wrongdoer, but he changes his mind and breaks-off the illegal act/attack -- your continuing the attack makes **you** the initial attacker in the eyes of the law. Beware! Just because he started the thing, doesn't necessarily give you the right to finish it.

> QUESTION: Hey, you're really getting me nervous. You mean that if I use a firearm to defend myself, I may get arrested?
>
> ANSWER: Unfortunately, that's a possibility, unless you have a responding police officer who also believes in your God-given Right to self-defense. On the other hand, you will be alive. Your wife will be alive. Your kids will be alive. The other alternative (lying dead on the ground) sure leaves alot to be desired.

DUTY TO RETREAT UNLESS AT HOME OR OFFICE:

I need to add here that the use of deadly physical force has a qualifier. To use it -- you must reasonably believe it's necessary to prevent the imminent commission of a forcible felony and/or to save yourself or another from great bodily harm or death (where you and/or that person has a legal right to do so). Also, you have an absolute duty to retreat if you are not inside your home, or business, or on the curtilage[151] of your dwelling, and you can retreat or escape with reasonable safety. This is normally referred to as the "retreat rule", or "castle doctrine". Again, this only applies to the use of deadly force. You have no duty to retreat when lawfully using non-deadly force, no matter where you are.

How does this retreat rule apply to stopping a forcible felony **not** inside your home or inside your business? That's a tough question, because the courts can't seem to make their minds up on this, either. I can only give you my best guess:

If by safely retreating you can stop the forcible felony -- you probably have to retreat. Otherwise, you can use deadly physical force (ie: shoot the bastard) only if it appears reasonably necessary to stop the felony. If there's another equally reasonable way to stop it -- you may have to go the other route. It's sometimes a hard question, and almost always is a jury issue -- and most jurors will go your way if it was a judgment call. But then, nobody really knows what a jury will do.

However, the real exception to this retreat rule is when you are in your own home or inside your business. If this is the case you may stand your ground -- unless (of course) the other person has an equal right to be on the property. If that's the situation -- it's back to the retreat doctrine again. Remember, if you're only a guest — you must retreat if you can.

There's a recent exception to this, which seems to apply only to your home. It isn't well-drafted, and I'm sure it will be challenged in court. It came out of a domestic violence case where the Florida Supreme Court decided that you shouldn't have to flee your own home if you were a domestic violence victim. Unfortunately, the new jury instruction sounds like it changed the law more favorably to abuse victims — but it really didn't. In fact, it made it worse. Here's the jury instruction which took effect in mid-1999:

> If the defendant was attacked in [his/her] own home, or on [his/her] own premises, by a co-occupant [or any other person lawfully on the premises] [he/she] had a duty to retreat to the extent reasonably possible without increasing [his/her] own danger of death or great bodily harm. However, the defendant was not required to flee [his/her] home and had the lawful right to stand [his/her] ground and meet force with force even to the extent of using force likely to cause death or great bodily harm if it was necessary to prevent death or great bodily harm to [himself/herself].

Why didn't it change anything?

Because you still have to retreat if you reasonably can. That's the old instruction. Hasn't changed a thing there.

Why did it make it worse?

Because the instruction now seemingly applies not only to co-occupants, but also to anybody else lawfully on the premises. That wasn't the intent of the Supreme Court! How did that get in there?

Does that mean your drunken date who you allowed to sleep over on the couch, who suddenly goes berserk and attacks you with a knife? How about the salesman you invite in who decides rape or pillage is a better line of work? Obviously, I would hope not — but that's what it seems to say.

Unfortunately, I think the drafters of this instruction inadvertantly screwed-up. But, the instruction is there — until the courts get around to correcting it — and realizing what happened. Test case time, again.

Anyway, back to self-defense in general.

What constitutes your home or business? Well, if you are at work inside your employer's premises, you may stand your ground. If you are a guest in someone's home, you may stand your ground. If you are inside your own business premises, you may stand your ground. If you are in a hotel or motel room you have legally rented, you may stand your ground.[152] Likewise, in your own home or dwelling, subject to the possible exceptions in the new jury instruction. But remember, these exceptions to the retreat rule always depend upon your having a superior right to be on the premises than the attacker, and you still must act reasonably.

Thus, if the wife comes at you with a knife in the house, and you can run out the back door, you gotta run.

Why?

Because she has an equal right to be in the house (Yeah! Even if you are the one who pays the mortgage!) If you're in a wheelchair, and obviously can't make it -- shoot her! However, your in-laws may never speak to you again! (This may, or may not be an added benefit). And ladies, if you have a restraining order and hubby decides to break-in the old homestead to teach you a major lesson with a baseball bat -- take the .357 and fire away -- if needed, because he no longer has an equal right to be there, as long as the restraining order prevents him from coming into the house while you are there. The new jury instruction does not apply.

Now, remember that this last paragraph, as with all these explanations are subject to somebody else's passing judgment on whether your actions were reasonable, or not. So, don't think that just by following this book you are safe -- because you're not. It will always depend, no matter how clear you think it may be.

seems that   according to inner-city gang etiquette, if you flee, they "lose face". So, they have to shoot you so they don't lose their reputation. Wonderful, huh?

The same danger zone exists with a guy coming at you with a knife. When he gets within 20 feet of you, you have only a couple of seconds before he can close the distance, and stab you.[153] Very little time to make a safe escape. Of course, if you're in a car, and you know that all he has is a knife -- you can probably escape with safety, unless you're stuck in traffic.

QUESTION: If a person comes on my curtilage after I tell him not to, can I shoot him?

ANSWER: The normal rule is only if you have a reasonable fear of death or great bodily harm; or he is in the commission of a "forcible felony"; or if you are resisting the commission of any other felony upon your own person, or in or upon any dwelling house which you are in, and it appears there is no other reasonable way to stop the felony from proceeding.[154] Of course, all this is still subject to being negated if you used "excessive force", and what seems O.K. to you may not seem O.K. to a jury. Thus, you'd better read the endnote I just cited to in this answer, as well as the previous section on excessive force. In other words, I don't advise it.

DEADLY FORCE -- USE TO PREVENT ESCAPE:

A citizens right to prevent an escape is not as broad as a police officers. It is a dangerous area to get into since a mistake can lead to criminal, and civil repercussions. Basically, you can use any reasonable force that you reasonably believe is necessary to prevent the escape of a person who is under arrest, and was in your custody.[155]

I wouldn't suggest that it's a reasonable use of force to shoot somebody who is trying to escape from a non-violent felony or misdemeanor. Even if it were legal, the hassle that you'd probably go through afterwards would rarely be worth it. And remember, that once this guy is running in the other direction, you are rarely in physical danger. If you shoot him, and a jury decides that was the use of "excessive force", you've just committed an aggravated battery, or manslaughter.[156]

Law enforcement and correctional officers were granted an exception from the definition of "deadly force" where they use "less-lethal munition" in good faith, and within the scope of their duties. This is a 1999 amendment to F.S. 776.06. Less lethal munition is defined as a projectile that is designed to stun, temporarily incapacitate, or cause temporary discomfort to a person without penetrating the person's body. Thus, the good faith use of such ammunition by an officer will be considered the use of "non-deadly force". This statute does not apply to a citizens use of such ammunition, although it raises the question.

So again, what is excessive force? Well, it depends on what everybody else decides was reasonable under the facts and circumstances. And again, this boils down to the attitude of the responding police officers, who your lawyer is, and what kind of jury you get. Not a necessarily pleasant experience since the line between being a hero, and being sued, or arrested yourself -- is very thin.

QUESTION: So, when could I use deadly force involving an escape?

ANSWER: Unless you're a police officer, it's a tough question. My opinion is that anytime it's a rape, armed robbery, homicide, arson, non-parental kidnapping, or bombing, (or the attempt) and the guy refused to stop after a warning, assuming a warning is practical. These situations are so serious that society would have a hard time faulting you.[157] As to anything else -- it's gonna depend.

QUESTION: How about non-deadly force, like a Taser, stun gun, mace, or something similar?

157

ANSWER: If it involves a felony, I personally feel this would
be more than reasonable to stop an escape. If it's
a misdemeanor, I really don't know, and would
probably advise to stay away from it, just because
of the civil liability side, no matter what the law is.

SOME OF THE POSSIBLE CRIMES AND PENALTIES FOR EXCESSIVE FORCE:

Uh, oh! Here comes the real bad news! What happens when you screw-up, make a mistake, or are just an unfortunate victim of circumstances. The name of the game is punishment. You and your legislators are screaming for penalties and jail time -- but everybody forgot to put some protections in for those of us who are using self-defense, and who mistakenly go over the line, however slight. A person who is justified in using force, but goes too far should not ordinarily be facing the penalties that exist today, but he or she does. Here's the scoop.

MANSLAUGHTER:

Manslaughter is the killing of another human being by culpable negligence, without lawful justification. It also occurs when there is a use of excessive force. Manslaughter is a second degree felony which is ordinarily punishable by up to fifteen years in the prison system.

Since this legal definition may be somewhat confusing, let me explain it a bit simpler by breaking it into its components. Basically, I meant that manslaughter happens one of two principal ways. Method one is called "culpable negligence". Culpable negligence is more than simple negligence, it is conduct so gross and flagrant that it amounts to a reckless disregard of human life, or is conduct done with such a want of care as to raise the presumption of a conscious indifference to the consequences. It must be of such a nature that the defendant knew, or reasonably should have known that the act or inaction was likely to result in death or great bodily injury to another.

The second way it occurs is where you misjudge the law or the facts involved in self-defense or legal justification. If you do, and you also wind-up killing someone -- the crime is manslaughter. One way this happens is if you do have the legal right (ie: "justification") to use force, but in doing so you "unnecessarily" kill another. What do I mean by "unnecessarily"?

Well, that is kind of self-explanatory. It means that you acted in a manner disproportionate to the act, or took a life where there was no reasonable necessity for doing so. I use the word "<u>reasonable</u>" necessity, because deciding what is reasonable doesn't always mean you were right. You may have been wrong to use the degree of force you did, but if this seemed to be reasonable under the circumstances -- you would still be legal, and should not be subject to prosecution.

AGGRAVATED ASSAULT:

The most common case I defend that is related to a self-defense situation that has supposedly gone wrong -- is aggravated assault.[158] Aggravated assault is a third degree felony that carries a three (3) year mandatory minimum prison sentence if a firearm or destructive device was involved. F.S. 775.087(2). By mandatory prison sentence -- we mean that if convicted, you've got to serve the prison portion, even if the judge doesn't feel you deserve it. He just has no choice.

So, what is an aggravated assault? Well, to understand, you first have to know the definition of an assault.

An assault is an intentional, unlawful threat done by word or act, to do violence to another person, coupled with the apparent ability to do so, and by doing some act that creates a well-founded ("reasonable") fear in the other person that the violence is imminent (to be "immediate"). To make an assault "aggravated" -- the assault must be committed with a deadly weapon, without any intent to kill, or must be done with an intent to commit a felony.

Thus, the key elements of an assault are:

a. An intentional threat
b. That is unlawful
c. To do violence against another
d. By doing some act
e. Which act creates a reasonable fear in the other person
f. That the violence is imminent (ie: "immediate").

How does an aggravated assault typically happen in a self-defense context?

Well, let's say your neighbor's kid keeps running over your lawn with his truck at high speed. This is dangerous. This is a breach of the peace. This is a trespass. This is criminal mischief. This stinks! Everytime you call the cops -- they arrive twenty minutes after all is done and over, and they can never catch the kid. Plus, they can't arrest him for a misdemeanor not done in their presence. That's the law, and it really stinks! It also needs to be corrected.

You're frustrated as hell. You're also rightfully worried that your dog, kid, wife, etc. -- will eventually get run-over by this nut. You're probably right.

Rather than call me for innovative legal advice,[159] you decide to save a buck, confront the stupid bastard, and make an impression he won't forget. Surely, who could blame you?

The magic day arrives, and as junior begins to zero-in at high-speed, you raise your mighty 12 gauge in his direction.

Suddenly, an amazing change in attitude is noticed, and junior turns his truck in the opposite direction as fast as he can. However, since he hates your guts, anyway, he calls the cops. Maybe he calls daddy or mommy -- who can't understand why anyone would point a gun at dear, darling junior -- but the end result is always the same -- you're charged with aggravated assault!

Unless you find an understanding prosecutor, a super jury, a really good attorney, or a combination of all the above -- you're going to jail for three years!

Incredible, isn't it? I mean, we all know who should be going to jail -- and it sure ain't you -- but that's the way it goes. Moreover, even if you get the charge reduced -- you stand a very good chance of losing your right to own and possess firearms ever again!

A SELF-DEFENSE STATUTE NEEDED FOR CITIZENS:

Is there no justice? Probably not -- but that's your fault for allowing the legislature to pass such laws without providing for intelligent exceptions. What we really need is a statute that says something to the effect of:

> "No person who honestly believes he is acting in self-defense, or lawful justification, even if mistaken, shall be subject to an enhanced or mandatory sentence because of the use of a firearm or dangerous weapon unless such a sentence is recommended by a jury or the trier of fact, or upon a plea, when such defense is found to be without any logical basis. In any such instance, the burden shall be upon the defendant by a preponderance of evidence."

A statute so worded would allow a judge or jury to decide what sentence is fair, rather than taking it out of their hands. If you agree -- write your state senator and representative. Do something you can be proud of. Heck, that's what being a citizen is all about!

EXCUSABLE HOMICIDE:

Excusable homicide is not a crime. It is a defense.[160] You can't be convicted of manslaughter or murder if the homicide is legally excusable.[161]

QUESTION: You mean there are actually times when I can kill somebody, and legally get away with it?

ANSWER: Well, the answer is that "accidents happen", and as tragic as it may be, if a death results from an accident that falls short of culpable negligence -- it's not considered murder or manslaughter, as the conduct is legally excusable.

QUESTION: Why?

ANSWER: Probably because our Constitution has a requirement that the punishment must not be disproportionate to the act being punished, and convicting somebody of murder or manslaughter for a total accident, or simple negligence, is a bit too much for most courts. That doesn't mean that that's the end of it, because I can guarantee you that somebody is gonna get sued in civil court --

and the suit will be for "big time" damages. But, at least there shouldn't be (the key here is "shouldn't be") any criminal charge for a homicide.

If you'd like some examples of excusable homicide, I'll pick a few from the law books that actually happened. The classic case is two kids cleaning, or looking at a loaded weapon. It drops, and somehow goes off. Another scenario is a hunting accident where culpable negligence is not involved.

However, the definition of excusable homicide is much broader than this, and can act as a total, or as a partial defense (which could allow a homicide to be downgraded to a lesser charge). In order to understand this, you need to know the legal definition of "excusable homicide.[162] The definition follows:

Homicide is excusable when:

(1)   Committed by accident and misfortune in doing any <u>lawful</u> act by <u>lawful</u> means with usual <u>ordinary</u> caution, and <u>without</u> any unlawful intent; or

(2)   When done by accident or misfortune in the heat of passion, upon any sudden and sufficient provocation; or

(3)   When done upon a sudden combat, without any dangerous weapon being used, and not done in a cruel or unusual manner.

Subsection (1) we've already discussed. Subsections (2) and (3) are actually pretty similar in execution. They both involve situations where a fight or heavy duty verbal argument is (usually) occurring. In subsection (2) the death must be accidental upon a sudden and sufficient provocation. In subsection (3) it is upon a sudden combat, without any dangerous weapon being used, and not done in a cruel or unusual manner. Thus, the third section protects a person who becomes involved in a fight which accidentally leads to the death of the other party, if the other conditions are met.[163]

There aren't alot of examples of these cases around. In fact, most of the court decisions explain why the facts do <u>not</u> constitute an excusable homicide. However, I will give you the few examples that have managed to be decided. Please remember, that if you change the facts in these cases only slightly, the result could be just the opposite of what occurred.

Typical, are two people in a normal fist-fight, and a normal blow causes an unexpected death to the other. Another example is one man pushing another in a verbal dispute, and the other man suffering a heart attack, and dying. Last, but not least, is one man pushing another, with the other falling, and unexpectedly landing on an object that killed him.

Obviously, these cases could be decided differently if you change the facts only slightly. For instance, if you knew the other guy had a bad heart -- you might have a real problem. So too, if you saw that pointed object on the ground, and gave him a push in the right direction. And, if you were a karate expert looking for a vital spot that could cause such a result? Anyway, I think you get the point -- and the point is: Don't get involved in these things in the first place. Buy a large, intelligent dog, and have <u>him</u> take care of things for you.

DEFENSES TO CIVIL LIABILITY (C.776.085):

It is a complete defense to any civil action for damages against you if you prove that the injured person was injured during the commission or attempted commission of a forcible felony (not the escape from). This defense can alternatively be shown by proof that the injured person was convicted of the forcible felony.

QUESTION: What if you use excessive force?

ANSWER: Darn if I know, although my guess is that you will still be OK, unless the other guy surrendered, and you shot him, anyway. That's because the crime would be over — and you'd be the new aggressor. Again, there are no reported Florida cases on this question, and it's a hard one to answer. Time for that exciting test case, again.

OTHER CIVIL PROBLEMS:

INSURANCE:

The first thing you need to know is that you are probably not covered by your insurance policy for anything that involves self-defense, defense of property, or preventing a forcible felony. Your Homeowners insurance does not cover it because your act is generally not one of negligence -- but instead is an "intentional" act which is normally excluded in almost all insurance policies. This probably won't apply if the weapon goes off accidentally in a struggle, because an accident would imply "negligence" or an "unintentional act" that should be within your coverage.[164]

Now, you may say that a jury would never award damages against you for defending your life or property -- but in a 1989 in a Florida Supreme Court case, State Farm v. Marshall, the Supreme Court affirmed a $575,000.00 verdict in favor of a person who broke into the Defendant's home and attacked him.[165] In its Opinion, the Court not only upheld the jury verdict, but also held that the Homeowners policy did not cover any part of this since the act of intentional self-defense was involved.

Incredible! How the heck a jury could ever come up with this result is beyond me, but it happened! And, you'd better be aware that if it happened once, it can happen again. Anything is possible in the law!

So, what can you do about it? You can try the impossible, which is finding an insurance company that will accept a rider to your policy that states something to the effect of: "Despite any wording to the contrary, this policy covers any act by any insured performed in self-defense on or immediately about the insured property." However, don't bet on finding one that will do it.

On the other hand, assuming that you somehow luck-out, and do find such an amazing company, would you please call me with their name and address, because I've been looking for one for a long time, and so have a lot of other people.

A SUMMARY ON THE USE & DISPLAY OF WEAPONS:

On a technical note, remember that there's a distinction between "deadly force", and a "deadly weapon". There is also a difference between the "display" and "use" of any weapon, deadly or not. Thus, the "display" of a deadly weapon, without its discharge, by an ordinary citizen will normally be considered the use of a "deadly weapon", but it will only be considered the use of "non-deadly force".[166]   In other words, just because it's a deadly weapon doesn't mean it's also the use of deadly force unless it's discharged.   While that may not seem real important -- it is.

Why?

Well, since you only have the right to use any reasonable "non-deadly force" against a misdemeanor -- you may have a defense to the display of the weapon -- assuming a jury finds that you acted reasonably. Obviously, a very important question if you're charged with aggravated assault, and are facing a three year mandatory prison sentence.

Thus, you need to remember as far as a firearm or deadly weapon is concerned: you can only threaten its immediate use to: (1) prevent death, (2) prevent great bodily harm, (3) stop a felony from being perpetrated upon yourself, (4) stop a forcible felony from being perpetrated on yourself or another, or (5) stop a felony that is being committed inside, or to a dwelling where you're at. It should also be legal if you have placed a person under arrest for a felony.   Otherwise, your threat of the immediate use of a deadly weapon could be considered to be "unreasonable", and perhaps the use of "excessive force". If that happens, you are going to be charged with, and probably be found guilty of aggravated assault. At a minimum, it's improper exhibition. Of course, causing physical injury to someone by the use of a deadly weapon, or deadly force is also subject to the question of excessive force, independent of the display of the weapon.

QUESTION: How could is it possible to use deadly force without a deadly weapon?

ANSWER: Well, I'll give you an example. If you were trying to stop a person from committing a grand theft, and grabbed him by the throat until you choked him to death -- there would be no deadly weapon involved -- but you certainly would have used deadly force. Obviously, lots of other examples could be thought of.

QUESTION: Using that last example -- is there any way that that might be legal?

ANSWER: Well, let's try the example method, again. Let's say that the guy refuses to let go of whatever he's stealing, and you keep choking him until he stops struggling. Unfortunately for him, he dies. It should be excusable homicide, or justifiable use of force in that circumstance. Test case time.

QUESTION: So, when should I use a deadly weapon?

ANSWER: This is opinion time. In my opinion, you should only display it when you feel it's necessary to stop the commission of a forcible felony, or to prevent death or great bodily harm. Otherwise, the risks are too great, even if you are legal.

QUESTION: What if three guys surround me, and say they're gonna beat me up?

ANSWER: It depends. If their motive is robbery, or another forcible felony -- you're legal. If they just want to do some bodily damage, the answer is "no", unless they've made it clear that you'll be hospital material afterwards, and you believe it. Same thing if they don't tell you their motive, but it's reasonable to believe it's hospital or felony time. If you've got a weak heart, and won't survive -- I'd warn them of your condition before I did anything. If you don't know what the hell they want -- maybe. However, don't get "macho" just because you have a gun. This is why some people who use guns go to jail -- and should. Moreover, the legal consequences of using deadly force, no matter how justified you were, are just not worth it, if it's avoidable.

QUESTION: Didn't you just tell me that I could legally display a firearm if I didn't discharge it?

ANSWER: No! I said that you <u>might</u> be able to do it, and it <u>might</u> be legal — because mere display, even coupled with a threat to use it, is normally the use of "non-deadly force". But — you also <u>might</u> get arrested. You also <u>might</u> have a jury decide that the display was not reasonable. In other words, "might" doesn't necessarily mean "right", in this scenario. It's always better to be on the safe side unless you're sure that the alternative is death, great bodily harm, or a serious felony!

QUESTION: What other situations do you see where people get in trouble?

ANSWER: Well, there are several types of cases that seem to come up, again-and-again, with slight factual variations — I'll give you a few in the next section.

SELF-DEFENSE CASES THAT GO WRONG OR RIGHT:

Situation Number One -- Road Warriors:

The worst place to display a weapon is in the heat of a traffic jam, or somebody cutting you off. Tempers seem to flare, and as he cuts you off, tailgates you, or whatever — you do it right back. Eventually, it escalates to the point of you taking out your handgun, and displaying it — usually without pointing it. You've shown him that you're armed — and not to push his luck.

Whether justified or not -- it's usually a very bad decision! You should have used the cellular, backed-off, and realized this guy was a low-life, hateful, egg-sucking, moron — instead, you're now the moron. What's worse is that the jerk now has the opportunity to "really" get even, and will call the police, and lie about what happened. He'll say you pointed the gun at him, and that he was in fear of being shot. Moreover, one he says that — he's stuck himself to the story, or he may get in trouble for a false police report.   He'll also leave out the fact that he almost killed you several times with his car, and that your gun was pointed skyward. In fact, he'll probably get immense satisfaction from your unjustified arrest, and prosecution. If you're real lucky, he may realize somewhere down the line that you don't deserve a three year mandatory sentence, and may tell the truth — or may tell the prosecutor that he doesn't mind if they "plea bargain" the case to something less.

So remember, rarely will you be in a position that displaying a firearm in a vehicle is anything but a really bad move. Only if you reasonably think you're about to be highjacked, or robbed is this advisable. I guess if he was trying to ram you, and you weren't trying to ram back, the same would apply. But otherwise, remember that you can normally pull over, and let him go by — thereby avoiding it all. If you can avoid it, you should.

Situation Number Two -- What's that gonna do against this:

Remember what I told you about escalation? It tends to get worse and not better.

Typical scenario is you get in a verbal confrontation with someone, and rather than walk away — you take out your pepper spray. The next thing you know — the guy has his gun out saying: "What's that gonna do against this?" Very serious situation. An apology, or backoff is usually the safer method of conduct, even if you were in the right, and do have to swallow your pride.

Situation Number Three -- Get the hell off my property:

This usually is justified, but nobody believes you. You have a trespasser, or somebody on your property who doesn't belong there. You take your gun with you for "just in case". This is totally legal when you're on your property. You never point the thing at him, but you make darn sure he knows it's there. He, being the wonderful person that he is, makes that 911 call telling the police that you pointed the gun at him, and threatened to blow him away unless he left your property. The police arrest you.

Sometimes this guy honestly believes you pointed the gun at him. Sometimes it's purely a crock. Sometimes you over-reacted. But, usually, you were well within your rights. Whatever, you now have a problem if he didn't tell the complete truth. If he did, then the police shouldn't be arresting you because you do nothing wrong by going armed on your own property. I mean . . . if you were right . . . what are you gonna do? Ask the armed robber to wait while you go and get your gun? On the other hand, let's hope you didn't threaten to shoot him if he didn't leave. This would not be a real good move unless he was in the commission of a forcible felony. I guess you just need to use good judgment. Personally, if I were in this situation, I'd try to hide the gun in a pocket, or under a jacket so the other person didn't know it was there. That way, I'd have the element of surprise if I needed it.

Situation Number Four -- South Florida Armed and Ready:

Well, I've given you all the bad scenarios -- here's the other one that I've heard over-and-over that always works out for the best. It happens in driveways, in shopping malls, and in gas stations. Nobody reports it to the police because they're scared they'll get arrested. It goes something like this:

You pull into a gas station late at night. Suddenly, a car pulls up next to you, and three or four very scary looking dudes appear ready to do you in some very serious fashion. You calmly display your handgun, pointed upwards — and they drive away just as suddenly as they came. You wipe away the sweat, and thank God for the handgun. You think about calling the police, and then think better of it. Very typical. You did the right thing all around — especially in South Florida.

There are other cases I see — but these are the most common. I hope the examples can be of some help, but every situation is different. There are no set answers for anything.

A SUMMARY ON SELF-DEFENSE LAW:

In summation of this chapter I repeat the same old major warning as before. Was your action reasonable? Was it necessary? Maybe to you it was -- but what will a police officer, prosecutor, or jury say later? Hmmmm! That's the problem! That's why these laws are dangerous to the average citizen. Moreover, if you are only permitted to use non-deadly force, and exceed that by displaying and threatening the use of a deadly weapon, or engaging in the use of deadly force -- you may be charged with of aggravated assault, even if you don't fire a shot, shoot an arrow, or throw that hatchet.

So, to summarize this section, when can you use deadly force? Hmmm, tough question. The answer? Well, truthfully -- whenever you're not prosecuted for it.

And when will that be, you ask?

169

Probably, if it's a life or death situation, or it looks like it. Probably, if somebody is already using a firearm or deadly weapon against you, and escape could be hazardous or risky. Probably, if someone breaks into your house, and you just don't want to take the risk of telling him to drop the weapon, because if you do -- he's got the drop on you. And probably, if there is a robbery of your business involving the display of a firearm or other deadly weapon by one of the perpetrators.

These are classic cases of where people are usually not prosecuted -- but as said before: There are no guarantees!

WHAT TO DO AFTER THE POLICE ARRIVE:

I've done alot of speaking engagements since I first wrote this book, and everybody seems to ask me the following question: "What should I do if I've shot someone in self-defense?"

Well, first of all -- take my business card, you're gonna need it -- and call me, or another qualified criminal attorney before you make any detailed statement to the police. However, if it happened outside don't drag the body inside, like everyone tells you to. That's the worst thing you could possibly do. With modern crime scene technology, you'll already be branded a liar, and it will go downhill from there. Don't disturb the scene, to whatever extent that is possible. Don't get rid of, or destroy evidence. That will also go against you.

Next, remember that "anything you say can, and will, be used against you." While many attorneys tell their clients not to say anything, I go along with a modified version of that. I think it's extremely important that the police realize that the body on the floor in the pool of blood is NOT the victim! You're the victim! In order to make sure the officer knows this, something akin to the following statement is extremely pertinent:

"Officer, I was attacked by this man, and thought he was armed.[167] I was in fear for my life, and was forced to shot him in self-defense."

Once you've said this, and you're sure he's heard it -- you don't generally want to go into any specifics until you've spoken to a really good lawyer who knows this stuff. Specifics can get you into deep trouble, even if your act was one hundred per cent perfectly legal.

Why?

Well, obviously, you're nervous as hell, and fourteen million different thoughts are racing through your head, all at the same time. If ever you're gonna screw something up, get it twisted and out of place, or leave out an important detail -- this is it! Moreover, even though you know what happened, you haven't gotten your thoughts together, yet -- and you don't know how to say what happened in the "right way".

Now, I don't mean that by the "right way" you've made something up. That's not the way I do business. On the other hand, you can say the same thing ten different ways -- and only one of them is gonna walk you out of that courtroom. That's why you want to speak to your lawyer. So he can go over the entire thing with you, and make sure you know what to say -- and more importantly -- what not to say.

Yes, you want to make sure the police know that it was self-defense; that you were in fear of your life; that he was the attacker, and that he was armed -- or you thought he was. But, beyond that is dangerous, and anything you say (other than wanting an attorney) will probably screw your case up, later.

Most police officers who are on your side will not push the point, and will almost lead you into saying it was self-defense, you were in fear for your life, and you want to talk your lawyer before you say anything else. However, if they want details -- beware! Tell them that you'll be glad to talk to them once you've had a chance to calm down, and have spoken to your lawyer. If they're on your side -- that will normally satisfy them. If it doesn't satisfy them, they're probably looking to make an arrest -- and that's certainly not on your side..

Moreover, if they're gonna arrest you -- they're gonna arrest you! Giving them a detailed story isn't going to change anything -- you'll still wind-up in a cell. So, if you follow my advice, at least you won't have screwed it up for yourself later on.

911 — USE IT!

The best thing you can ever do if you think you're being attacked, broken into, or about to be attacked, etc. -- is call 911. Tell them you're frightened! Tell you think the guy may be armed (even if you're not sure -- it's certainly not a lie in this day and age). Tell them to hurry up and send somebody!

All this is being recorded! It's gonna be used as evidence in your favor! If the police don't get there in a few minutes, call 911 again! It's gonna be recorded again! The jury is going to wonder what the heck the police were doing while you were beginning to panic out while trying to defend home and family. Moreover, when the police do get there -- you're already the victim! They're going out there to rescue you! The dead son-of-a-bitch on the floor in the congealing pool of blood is the "bad guy" -- you're just the poor victim who luckily managed to save himself . . . and in the process, you performed a valuable civic service. Now, they have one less criminal on the street! Good job!

So, thank heaven for 911 -- if you use it.

CELLULAR PHONES — YOUR BEST DEFENSE:

Of course, if you're on the road, the same thing goes for cellular phones. When in a vehicle, or anywhere where a regular phone is not handy -- they are your best defense against the nut cases that inherit our streets and highways. If someone is doing strange things, dial 911 or *FHP, just so you have a record of your fear -- in case it really happens.

If you're lucky, they may send a unit to check it out before it happens. If not, at least we know who the victim is, and who the bad guy is. Very important factors in analyzing who gets sued, who gets arrested, or both.

On the other hand, please don't say that "I'm gonna shoot him if he comes in" -- even if you intend to. That's just asking for trouble. You want to make sure that they know you're scared. If you aren't, then there's something wrong with you, no matter how controlled you may be. Moreover, you certainly don't want to give the 911 operator the impression that you're gonna blow this guy away no matter what happens.

That just sounds like you're looking for trouble, and want to perform a "legal execution".

That's not what you want to do, in fact, you really want to give the impression that you'll only use your weapon as a "<u>last resort</u>". Try remembering that.

GETTING STOPPED BY THE POLICE:

What are your rights when the police stop you? Do you have to tell them you've got a gun on you, etc.? Interesting questions.

As a general rule — you have no obligation to tell a police officer you have a gun or weapon on you, or in your vehicle. However, you may commit a crime if you lie to them about it. Therefore, my rule of thumb is to <u>never volunteer</u> that information unless the officer is about to look into the glove compartment, etc. — where he will obviously find it. Other than that — keeping your mouth shut on the issue is probably the best approach.

However, if asked — you need to make a decision on whether to answer the question directly — or not. You could legally say: "Officer, I have absolutely nothing illegal on me, or in my vehicle. And, unless I'm being arrested — I don't think your question is proper." However, if you do that — you may not like the reaction you get. It all depends who you are — and who he/she is. It also depends on why you're being stopped.

I think the best approach on being specifically asked is usually to say something that "legalizes" your position — ie — "Officer, I have a legal firearm securely encased in my vehicle." Or — "Officer, I have a concealed permit in my wallet. I also have a legally concealed firearm. Would you like to see the permit?"

Remember — officers are creatures of "respect". If they perceive your response as "disrespectful" — you're probably in for trouble. If you're unlucky enough to get an officer who likes to make trouble, or give a hard time — trouble it will be. So, use your best judgment under the circumstances — if you have to give up some of your constitutional rights to avoid jail — maybe that isn't the worst choice. You'll have to make your own decision. On the other hand — let me tell you — jail sucks, no matter how short the visit is.

On the other hand, if the officer discovers or is informed that you have a weapon or firearm — he has the right to temporarily take it into custody during the encounter to protect himself/herself from harm. Totally legal. The officer may even unload the weapon, and place it in his unit.

After the encounter — unless you're being arrested, your supposed to get the firearm or weapon back. Probably unloaded — until you or he leaves. Again — totally legal. Police don't want to get shot — that makes perfect sense to me.

NANOSECONDS TO REACT:

I've thought very hard about including this particular section in the book. As a trial attorney I read lots of cases, every day of the week. Many of these cases are frightening. They don't involve self-defense. They involve people who didn't use self-defense. People who didn't have time to defend themselves, didn't know how, or didn't have the weapons or knowledge to defend themselves. These people, for the most part — are now dead. They are murder victims, and worse. The excerpts I've taken from just a few of these cases are not for the weak of heart — but it's instructional. Maybe, they will not have died totally in vain if you read it, and learn something from it. Again, it's not a pretty sight. It's sad — and if you shed a tear, it's OK. I do, every time I read them.

Heynard v. State, 689 So. 2d 239 (Fla. 1996):

Around 10 p.m. on January 30, Lynette Tschida went to the Winn Dixie store in Eustis. She saw Henyard and a younger man sitting on a bench near the entrance of the store. When she left, Henyard and his companion got up from the bench; one of them walked ahead of her and the other behind her. As she approached her car, the one ahead of her went to the end of the bumper, turned around, and stood. Ms. Tschida quickly got into the car and locked the doors. As she drove away, she saw Henyard and the younger man walking back towards the store.

Ms. Lewis noticed a few people sitting on a bench near the doors as she and her daughters entered the store. When Ms. Lewis left the store, she went to her car and put her daughters in the front passenger seat. As she walked behind the car to the driver's side, Ms. Lewis noticed Alfonza Smalls coming towards her. As Smalls approached, he pulled up his shirt and revealed a gun in his waistband. Smalls ordered Ms. Lewis and her daughters into the back seat of the car, and then called to Henyard. Henyard drove the Lewis car out of town as Smalls gave him directions. The Lewis girls were crying and upset, and Smalls repeatedly demanded that Ms. Lewis "shut the girls up." As they continued to drive out of town, Ms. Lewis beseeched Jesus for help, to which Henyard replied, "this ain't Jesus, this is Satan." Later, Henyard stopped the car at a deserted location and ordered Ms. Lewis out of the car. Henyard raped Ms. Lewis on the trunk of the car while her daughters remained in the back seat. Ms. Lewis attempted to reach for the gun that was lying nearby on the trunk. Smalls grabbed the gun from her and shouted, "you're not going to get the gun, bitch." Smalls also raped Ms. Lewis on the trunk of the car. Henyard then ordered her to sit on the ground near the edge of the road. When she hesitated, Henyard pushed her to the ground and shot her in the leg. Henyard shot her at close range three more times, wounding her in the neck, mouth, and the middle of the forehead between her eyes. Henyard and Smalls rolled Ms. Lewis's unconscious body off to the side of the road, and got back into the car. The last thing Ms. Lewis remembers before losing consciousness is a gun aimed at her face. Miraculously, Ms. Lewis survived and, upon regaining consciousness a few hours later, made her way to a nearby house for help. The occupants called the police and Ms. Lewis, who was covered in blood, collapsed on the front porch and waited for the officers to arrive.   As Henyard and Smalls drove the Lewis girls away from the scene where their mother had been shot and abandoned,   Jasmine and Jamilya continued to cry and plead: "I want my Mommy," "Mommy," "Mommy." Shortly thereafter, Henyard stopped the car on the side of the road, got out, and lifted Jasmine out of the back seat while Jamilya got out on her own. The Lewis girls were then taken into a grassy area along the roadside where they were each killed by a single bullet fired into the head. Henyard and Smalls threw the bodies of Jasmine and Jamilya Lewis over a nearby fence into some underbrush.

The moral to this case is what police experts will tell you — in an abduction, you stand a better chance doing anything but getting in the car. Criminals who are out to rob you, are normally not going to abduct you. Abductions are usually reserved for murderers. Cooperation only places you in a remote area where help is impossible. Better to be shot where somebody may call an ambulance — than dead in the middle of a field. If you're alone — break and run. If you're armed — use your weapon once you're free of being grabbed, and possibly disarmed. Too many police officers have lost their lives because they tried to grapple with dangerous offenders — rather than break away, and distance themselves, first. You won't be of any help to anyone if you're disarmed, bound, gagged, stuffed in a trunk, and then murdered.

James v. State, 695 So. 2d 1229 (Fla. 1997):

Pearson stated that when the two met, James was on his way to visit Tim Dick, the victim's son, and his girlfriend, Nichole, who also lived nearby. They stopped and talked for about ten minutes and Pearson watched James ingest about ten "hits" of LSD on paper. James told Pearson he had been drinking at Todd Van Fossen's party, but he appeared sober to Pearson. After briefly visiting Tim Dick and

Nichole where he drank some gin, James returned to his room at Betty Dick's house. When he entered the house, James noticed that Betty Dick's four grandchildren were asleep in the living room. One of the children, Wendi, awoke briefly when James arrived. She observed that he was laughing and appeared drunk. James went to the kitchen, made himself a sandwich and retired to his room. Eventually, he returned to the living room where he grabbed Betty Dick's eight-year-old granddaughter, Toni Neuner, by the neck and strangled her, hearing the bones pop in her neck. Believing Toni was dead, he removed her clothes and had vaginal and anal intercourse with her in his room. Toni never screamed or resisted. After raping Toni, he threw her behind his bed. James then went to Betty Dick's bedroom where he intended to have sexual intercourse with her. He hit Betty in the back of the head with a pewter candlestick. She woke up and started screaming, "Why, Eddie, why?" Betty's screaming brought Wendi Neuner to the doorway of her grandmother's bedroom where she saw James stabbing Betty with a small knife. When James saw Wendi he grabbed her, tied her up, and placed her in the bathroom. Thinking that Betty was not dead, James went to the kitchen, grabbed a butcher knife and returned to Betty's room and stabbed her in the back. James removed Betty Dick's pajama bottoms, but did not sexually batter her. Covered with blood, James took a shower in the bathroom where Wendi remained tied up and then threw together some clothes and belongings. He returned to Betty's room and took her purse and jewelry bag before driving away in her car. James drove across the country, stopping periodically to sell jewelry for money.

What do you say about this one? First — if she had a gun, she could have used it. Nothing else would have worked. Other than that, if you associate with people who use drugs and alcohol — disaster may occur. Be forewarned!

Campbell v. State, 679 So.2d 720 (Fla. 1996):

Campbell rang the doorbell to the Bosler home at 2:15 p.m. on December 22, 1986, and when Billy Bosler answered the door, Campbell stabbed him a number of times. Billy's adult daughter, Sue Zann Bosler, heard the commotion and came to her father's aid, and Campbell stabbed her. Billy died, Sue Zann lived. Sue Zann's testimony about the murder began with her describing what happened when she came out of her bedroom at the parsonage, which was the home of her father, mother, and sister:

Q. You're indicating that your dad was in the doorway, a man was stabbing him?
A: Yes.

Q. What, if anything, did you do?
A. By the time I got, I was walking out towards him to help him. He was being stabbed so many times that he was collapsing to the floor.

Q. And what did you do as you approached this scene?
A. As I approached the scene I went forward to help and I must have screamed because he turned around and he was going to stab me in the front.

Q. When you say he, Sue Zann, who are you talking about?
A. The man who was stabbing my father.

Q. You turned around and he goes to stab you in the front?
A. Yes.

Q. What do you do?
A. I turned to the right like this and he stabbed me three times in the back.

Q. Where on your back did he stab you?
A. Once in my shoulder, the knife went approximately four inches into my flesh, once below my shoulder in the back and three inches in and right by my spine approximately two inches.

Q. After you were struck those three times, what did you do?
A. I was knocked to the floor on my knees.

Q. Okay. Did he continue stabbing you?
A. No.

Q. What was your father doing?
A. He was trying to get up on his knee to try to help me.

Q. When you last saw him, he was on his knees in the hallway?
A. He was trying to get on his knees.

Q. So he was trying to lift himself up?
A. Yes.

Q. Was he able to do that?
A. No.

Q. Did he start to crawl toward you?
A. No, he couldn't.

Q. And you're stabbed over here?
A. Yes.

Q. Your father starts to move towards you or tries to get up?
A. He is trying to still get up.

Q. What happens to him next?
A. After I was stabbed to the floor, dad was trying to get up and the man turned around and start stabbing dad in the back many times.

You know the answer to this last case, and so do I. Sue Zann needed a firearm, and needed to use it before she did anything else. Nanoseconds to react!

In fact, private citizens firearms use guns in self-defense 800,000 to 2.5 million times a year according to a study by Professor Gary Kleck, a noted criminologist at the Florida State University. In 80 or 90 percent of these cases no shots are fired — because the criminal flees! According to the study, at least half a million cases of lawful self-defense happen a year where the crime is stopped! [168]

Next time your legislators try taking away your firearms — tell them to get real. Only criminals benefit by firearm regulations. It protects them from honest citizens like you and I.

SENTENCING HELL 1999:

Every time you vote for a "law and order" candidate — you are sacrificing the liberty your forefathers died for over the generations, because we already have so much law and order — that we have passed the area of sensibility — and are turning into a totalitarian society. Our laws are killing us.

So, get ready for the bad news — mandatory sentences of draconian proportions. Sheer fright — for anyone with any degree of insight or commonsense. I voted Republican — and for Governor Bush, but I'm really shaking in my boots from what I've seen passed. This is not government — it is an Inquisition! These sentences have no exceptions. Make a mistake on a self-defense issue — and you are literally fighting for your life before the court. It's all in Chapter 99-12. Here goes:

There is a ten (10) year mandatory prison sentence for possession of a firearm or destructive device during any forcible felony, including aggravated stalking, and aggravated child/elder/disabled abuse. The exception is to aggravated assault, possession by a felon, and burglary of a conveyance. If a firearm is discharged — then the mandatory sentence is twenty (20) years in prison. This also applies to aggravated assault, drug trafficking, and burglary of a conveyance, along with the other forcible felonies. If a person suffers death or great bodily harm — the mandatory sentence is a minimum of twenty-five (25) years to a maximum of life. If you possessed a machine gun, or firearm with a magazine equipped with a magazine that is "capable" of holding 20 or more centerfire cartridges — and commit one of the enumerated felonies — you have a fifteen (15) year minimum sentence. Otherwise, the penalties are the same.

Where are the problems, you say?

OK — here's your answer.

First, if you misjudge a self-defense situation — you've probably committed an "aggravated assault". Three year minimum mandatory. Kiss the wife and kids goodbye unless you've got a sympathetic detective working the case, and a pro-self defense prosecutor, to boot. If you didn't want to hurt the varlet — and fired a warning shot — you're now facing a twenty (20) year mandatory sentence. Kiss the wife and kids goodbye. Also kiss any grandchildren goodbye. If you hit the bastard, and wound him — twenty five years to life. Probably a good point to consider suicide.

One thing you should notice immediately from this is — firing a warning shot is no longer a very good idea — even if it is a very good idea. What I mean by this is that sometimes — firing a warning shot is the act that saves both your life — and the stupid bastard's who is about to attack you. But, the Legislature doesn't want to know about that. Even though they haven't changed the law on when such may be "reasonable" or not — they've imposed some draconian punishments if somebody later decides you didn't do the right thing.

Again — that's why these mandatory laws are absolutely awful! They're fine if the guy is really a criminal — but for the marginal case, or the case of mistaken judgment — it's tragic! The judge has no discretion. The mandatory sentence must be imposed! And if the other side are good actors, or are out to get even — you're gonna pay the price, guilty or not. This is sad stuff — and yet it's happening every day.

What really makes it sad is that the person who just tried to break into your home, and held a club on you when you came out will probably tell the cops that he was just walking across your lawn when you came after him with a gun. A "crazy man". All he was doing was cutting across the lawn, and you held a gun on him saying he was trying to break in your house.   If this is a neighbor you've been having a problem with, I almost guarantee this is what he'll say — and sometimes the police aren't real concerned about who really did what -- they just want that felony arrest, and let the system "sort it out".

Now, you're facing three years in prison.   Never did anything illegal in your life. The prosecutor offers you a deal.   No jail — just probation. Are you gonna take it?

You bet you are!   When you look into the eyes of your wife and kids — they'll be no doubt what you're going to have to do.   Innocent or not — the odds are with the State.   If the kid's a good liar, and really wants to get you — it's even worse.   He may even bring some buddies in to lie.

And hey, and what if you fired a warning shot as he came at you with the club?   Now, it's twenty years!   Are you really thinking you're going to take this to a jury if they offer you a deal with two years in prison?   Even if you go to trial, and win — how much has it cost you in money, stress, and sleepless nights?   Have you lost your job?   Will you lose it?   Have you had to mortgage the house?   Has the wife left you after two years of trials and appeals? Very heavy duty stuff -- make no mistake about it.

Situation number two — also quite common.   You have an absolute right to keep and carry a firearm anywhere on your property. You hear something outside, grab your firearm just in case, and walk outside.   Your nosey, antagonistic neighbor sees you, says what are you doing with a gun, you tell them mind their own damn business — and they call up the police saying you threatened them with a gun.   And the police, who probably don't have much choice at that point, are forced to arrest you.

Doesn't happen?

I see it all the time.   One neighbor trying to "get even".   The fact that you'll go to jail for something you didn't do — is not even a real concern.   Life in America!   God Bless this Country!

Want another example more on the lines of a real criminal? Fine.

Some stupid kid drops off a friend who commits a residential burglary. The kid waits for his buddy not knowing what he is about to do, but soon finds out when he sees him break in the house. The kid has a firearm legally in the glove compartment, and now knowing what is happening, waits for his buddy to come out. He hears a police car coming, and when his buddy gets in the car they try to escape, but are caught. This kid is just an accessory, but he faces a ten year minimum prison sentence for having possession of the gun. For a career criminal — very good. For somebody in between — perhaps a total injustice. Hard to say — it depends. But there again, is the problem. Judges don't have discretion. The sentence is mandatory. If you fall one inch within the statutory definition of the crime, no matter what the degree of your involvement — you are in deep trouble. The fact that a jury has the right to come back anyway they want isn't real comforting when you know the Florida Supreme Court has <u>forbidden</u> juries from being told what the possible sentence is that might be imposed, or that they have the inherent right to "pardon" a defendant, or come back with a lesser sentenced than legally deserved — if a conviction, as charged, would be unfair. In fact — they are told just the opposite!

So, juries that used to do the "right thing" — have been severely hampered by the law, today. They aren't allowed to be told the power they actually possess.

Same problem with judges. The Legislature doesn't trust them to be fair -- so they've imposed a mathematical set of "Sentencing Guidelines" which a judge must follow, even if he thinks it's unfair. This is where we are currently at.

A NEEDED CONSTITUTIONAL AMENDMENT:

What we need is a constitutional amendment that would guarantee that a jury be told the possible penalty that might be imposed, and be further told they have the absolute right to "pardon" someone charged with a crime, or reduce the crime to a lesser one, if they feel that is appropriate. If that happened, these terrible sentencing laws would be counter-balanced by the commonsense of the jury. Until that happens — we're all in a lot of trouble. Here's my suggestion:

"No mandatory sentence shall be imposed in any criminal case unless the trier-of-fact approves of its imposition in the verdict, or where tried non-jury, in the judgment. A jury shall be informed as to the length of any possible mandatory sentence which may be imposed prior to deliberating, and that they have the absolute discretion not to impose it if any reasonable basis exists. The decision of the trier-of-fact on such issue is final, and not subject to an appeal except upon a showing that the government withheld material, and exculpatory evidence which may have affected the decision of the trier-of-fact on the imposition of the mandatory sentence."

I know it's probably not going to do any good — but, if you don't try, you'll never know, right? So, go write Governor Bush, and your State Representatives a letter saying you want this constitutional amendment placed on the ballot. You have my personal permission to photocopy this page of the book, and mail it to them. If we all do that, week-after-week, month-after-moth — who knows? Miracles have happened before, haven't they?

CONCLUSION:

Well, that's it for the book. Hopefully, you'll never have to experience any of the situations I've outlined in this last chapter. That is my wish for you, and for your family. It is also my wish for the future of this State, and our Great Nation. Good luck, and God bless.

The End

ENDNOTES

1. That Every Man Be Armed, by Stephen P. Halbrook, Chapter 3, The Independent Institute (1984). See also, The Bill of Rights in Modern America, edited by David J. Bodenhamer, Indiana University Press (1993).

2. That Every Man Be Armed, by Stephen P. Halbrook, Chapter 3, page 81, The Independent Institute (1984).

3. See, Rinzler v. Carson, 262 So.2d 661,668 (Fla. 1972).

4. While the anti-gunners seem very concerned about the "one life" that your firearm might take -- they are not very concerned about the lives it will save. Statistics establish that 650,000 to 1,000,000 citizens use firearms in legal self-defense every year. Moreover, armed citizens get involved in stopping crimes to a much higher degree than others, and will take the chance to assist others, only because they are armed. I hear about this all the time. So, don't swallow this "one life" garbage the anti-gunners are trying to feed you. In fact, if they put their money into firearms education like the NRA has -- they'd probably eliminate the very problem they are complaining about.

5. See, American Rifleman, Armed Citizens and Crime Control, July 1988. In fact, according to another part of the study by Professor Gary Kleck, armed citizens legally kill two to seven times the number of criminals killed by law enforcement officers, a year. They also administer legal, but non-fatal wounds to criminals in numbers of 8,700 to 16,600 per year. A revised study in 1993 changed the figures to the higher number cited in the text.

6. United States v. Lopez, 115 S.Ct. 1624 (1995)

7. Printz v. United States, 117 S. Ct. 2365 (1997)

8. Staples v. United States, 511 US 600 (1994)

9. See, State v. Mitchell, 20 FLW 753 (2DCA March 24, 1995) which held that legal fireworks were not destructive devices, although fireworks which exceeded the permitted explosive weight allowed in Chapter 791, Florida Statutes, could be, if used as a weapon, or used to destroy property.

10. F.S. 790.001(6)

11. A "weapon" is defined as an instrument of attack or defense in combat. State v. Houck, 1995 Fla. Lexis 43 (Fla. February 2, 1995). Whereas, a "deadly weapon" or "dangerous weapon" is one, taking into account the manner of use, is likely to produce death or great bodily harm. Smith v. State, 573 So.2d 306 (Fla. 1990); Lindsey v. State, 64 So. 501 (Fla. 1914); Clemons v. State, 37 So. 647, 649 (Fla. 1904).

12. F.S. 790.065 (12)(a)

13. F.S. 790.17

14. F.S. 790.18

15. While there is some debate on exactly what a dirk is, it is usually defined as a long dagger. A dagger, on the other hand,   is usually defined as a weapon with a narrow, pointed, double-edged tip that is used for stabbing.

16. In Clemons v. State, 37 So. 647 (Fla. 1904), the Defendant was convicted of second degree murder for using brass knuckles, which resulted in the death of a man. The court held that brass knuckles could be classified as a "deadly weapon" in this case because anytime a weapon, as used, produces death (or great bodily harm) -- it's a deadly weapon.

17. F.S. 790.22

18. F.S. 790.22(3) & (4)(a).

19. 18 USC 922 (x)

20. F.S. 790.17

21. In U.S. v. Moore, 109 F.3d 1456 (9CCA 97) the court held a purchase from a dealer for a child under 18 was an illegal "strawman" transaction even though it was not illegal under state law. I think the decision would have been different had the person been 18.

22. 18 USC 922(a)(3) & (a)(5)

23. Rentals should be restricted to dealers, since this is a business purpose, and the business of dealing in firearms is restricted to those possessing a federal license to do so.

24. 18 USC 922(a)(5)

25. 18 USC 922(a)(3)(A) & (5)(A)

26. Interestingly, F.S. 790.28, which allows a Florida resident to purchase a rifle or shotgun in any contiguous state to Florida, shouldn't really affect this interpretation in the least, because the Florida statute doesn't prohibit anything. From an interpretative standpoint, it appears that the drafters may have misunderstood the federal law -- which is certainly understandable if you ever try to read it. My interpretation on this was arrived at after several phone calls to ATF, to make sure I understood what the heck this part of the federal statute meant.

27. 18 USC 922 (b)(3)

28. F.S. 790.065(1)(a)

29. 18 USC 922(b)(3)(A)

30. "Intimate partner" means a present or former spouse; present or former cohabitating partner, or parent of a mutual child. 18 USC 921(32)

31. Domestic Violence section of 1994 Crime Bill, section 110401(8); 18 USC 921 (33); 18 USC 922 (b)(8).

32. 18 USC 922(g)(9)

33. F.S. 741.28 defines "domestic violence" as any form of assault, battery, stalking, including aggravated & sexual, or any criminal offense resulting in physical injury or death of one family or household member by another who is, or was residing in the same single dwelling unit.

34. It does apply to those who "manufacture" ammunition for sale.

35. F.S. 907.041(4) gives a list of "dangerous crimes", many of which are also "forcible felonies". These dangerous crimes include: arson, aggravated assault, aggravated battery, illegal use of explosives, child abuse, aggravated child abuse, abuse of elderly or disabled person or aggravated abuse thereof, hijacking, kidnap, homicide, manslaughter, sexual battery, robbery, carjacking, lewd, lascivious or indecent assault or act upon or in presence of child under 16, burglary of a dwelling, stalking, aggravated stalking, domestic violence under F.S. 741.28, home invasion robbery.

36. F.S. 948.03(1)(l). See, State v. Hart, 668 So.2d 589 (Fla. 1996).

37. W.J. v. State, 688 So.2d 954 (4DCA 1997); Williams v. State, 681 So.2d 817 (2DCA 1996).

38. F.S. 790.065(12)(d)

39. F.S. 790.065(12)(a)

40. F.S. 790.065(1)(a)

41. F.S. 790.065(7)

42. F.S. 790.065(12); 18 USC 922(a)(6)

43. Brady codified as 18 USC 922(s)

44. See also, Fla. Bd. Bar Examiners, 350 So.2d 1072 (Fla. 1977); In re Kastenbaum, 341 So.2d 503 (Fla. 1976).

45. Rice v. United States, 68 F.3d 702 (3CCA 1995).

46. F.S. 790.061

47. F.S. 790.06(1)

48. F.S. 790.06(12)

49. If the legislature wanted to cover everything, they probably would have included the "grounds" of the school, just as they did in F.S. 790.115(1)(ie: "on the grounds or facilities of any school"), or they would have defined it as "school plant" per F.S. 228.041(7), or "campus" per F.S. 228.091. Research of numerous Florida statutes shows similar definitions.   Compare, 18 USC 930.

50. 18 USC 930. "The term "Federal facility" means a building or part thereof owned or leased by the Federal government, where federal

employees are regularly present . . . ."

51. F.S. 790.06(1)

52. "Willful" under Florida law means: intentionally, knowingly, and purposefully. State v. May, 670 So.2d 374 (2DCA 1996). Under federal law it means that the person actually knew his conduct was illegal. Ratzlaf v. U.S., 510 US 135 (1994); U.S. v. Sanchez-Corcino, 85 F.3d 549 (11CCA 1996).

> "A thing is willfully done when it proceeds from a conscious motion of the will, intending the result which actually comes to pass. It must be designed or intentional, and may be malicious, though not necessarily so. "Willful" is sometimes used in the sense of intentional, as distinguished from "accidental," and, when used in a statute affixing a punishment to acts done willfully, it may be restricted to such acts as are done with an unlawful intent." Jersey v. Paper, 658 So. 2d 331 (Fla. 1995)

53. This is a chronic alcoholic whose mental process is permanently affected — not somebody who got intoxicated a few times — unless they've been convicted of two DUI's within 3 years.

54. This particular subsection allows revocation of the license in the discretion of the Dept. of State — it is not mandatory. F.S. 790.06(3).

55. Miami v. Swift, 481 So.2d 26 (3DCA 1985), jury award of $50,000 for the false arrest of a person with a gun in the console, was OK'd.

56. F.S. 790.053

57. F.S. 790.01

58. The term "manual possession" came from former F.S. 790.05, and means that the weapon is actually in your hand.

59. Dozier v. State, 662 So.2d 382 (4DCA 1995). Also, the term "ship" should be synonymous with the term "boat" in the sense of a motor boat, and a sail boat with a cabin. Since a "bicycle" has been excluded as a conveyance — I assume a canoe or similar type craft would also be excluded, but there is no case law..

60. A.M. v. State, 21 FLW 1957.

61. <u>F.S.</u> 790.001(16)

62. <u>Urquiola v. State</u>, 590 So.2d 497 (3DCA 1991)

63. <u>Alexander v. State</u>, 477 So.2d 557 (Fla. 1985)

64. <u>Gemmile v. State</u>, 20 FLW 816 (4DCA April 5, 1995)

65. <u>Bell v. State</u>, 636 So.2d 80 (2DCA 1994)

66. <u>Cates v. State</u>, 408 So.2d 797 (2DCA 1983)

67. Actually, this makes alot of sense. Since the key purpose of your Florida Constitutional right to keep and bear arms is for self defense, and since this is confirmed by both the "Declaration of Policy" in <u>F.S.</u> 790.25(1), and the constructions given to <u>F.S.</u> 790.25(4) & (5) -- it would be pretty silly to require the firearm to be difficult to access in an emergency. I mean, these things usually happen in a matter of seconds -- and you can't tell the bad guy to wait while you load your gun, or unlock your glove compartment. If you did, you'd already be dead.

Moreover, you might be interested in knowing that throughout the early history of this country, and well into the mid-Twentieth Century, many States allowed travelers to keep pistols in their vehicles, even if such was otherwise not permitted to the regular populace. In some part, this was due to the dangers associated with being waylayed while on the road. Sounds familiar, doesn't it?

This was certainly the rule in Florida. <u>See</u>, <u>Biennial Report of Attorney General</u>, January 12, 1933 (p. 628) & March 20, 1936 (p. 751); and <u>Opinion of Attorney General</u>, 051-105 (1951).

68. <u>F.S.</u> 790.053

69. Remember, if you can fire the weapon without physically opening, removing, or undoing the restraining device -- you're not legal -- because it's not "securely encased".

70. <u>F.S.</u> 790.001(15) states: "readily accessible for immediate use' means that a firearm or other weapon is carried on the person or within such close proximity and in such a manner that it can be retrieved and used as easily and quickly as if carried on the person."

71. <u>See</u>, <u>Ashley v. State</u>, 619 So.2d 294 (Fla. 1993).

72. <u>Boswink v. State</u>, 636 So.2d 584 (2DCA 1994).

73. <u>Watson v. Stone</u>, 4 So.2d 700, 702-703 (Fla. 1941).

74. 18 USC 926A

75. Again, I remind you that a "bicycle" is not a conveyance - and I doubt that a canoe, single man sailboat, or a rowboat would qualify, either because they would probably be considered purely "pleasure craft", and not really a functional conveyance. However, there are no court cases defining this.

76. <u>F.S.</u> 790.23 (3)(l)

77. <u>See</u>, <u>Sherrod v. State</u>, 484 So.2d 912 (3DCA 1986), where a conviction for carrying a concealed firearm was sustained because the defendant was on his apartment unit's parking lot when arrested -- a "common area".

78. <u>Caban v. State</u>, 475 So.2d 968 (4DCA 1985), held that a person's home or business in <u>F.S.</u> 790.25, refers to an individual's surrounding property as well as the buildings and structures situated thereon. This is not restricted to curtilage, for you can carry open or concealed, anywhere on your home or business property, although the retreat rule would certainly apply.

79. <u>Wassmer v. State</u>, 565 So.2d 856 (2DCA 1990); and <u>Turner v. State</u>, 645 So.2d 444 (Fla. 1994).

80. <u>F.S.</u> 790.25(3)(n)

81. <u>F.S.</u> 790.052

82. If you have a concealed permit, it's a second degree misdemeanor pursuant to <u>F.S.</u> 790.06(12). Otherwise, it's a first degree misdemeanor for a weapon, or a third degree felony for a firearm.

83. The primary case on this issue was <u>Wilson v. State</u>, 344 So.2d 1315 (2DCA 1977), <u>reh.</u> <u>denied</u>, 353 So.2d 679 (Fla. 1977); which held that it was reversible error for the judge not to instruct the jury that "knowledge

of the presence of the firearm" was essential to a conviction. <u>Accord</u>, <u>L.J. v. State</u>, 553 So.2d 286 (3DCA 1989); <u>V.B.L. v. State</u>, 408 So.2d 855 (3DCA 1982). In essence, you don't want to make a criminal out of someone who merely made a mistake, and carried it unwittingly. <u>See</u>, <u>Cole v. State</u>, 353 So.2d 952 92DCA 1978).

84. Recent studies have shown that these sprays can be ineffective against people on certain types of drugs, and against mentally unbalanced persons. I would guess that this might also apply against a highly motivated assailant. It's a good reason to remember that a spray will never replace a firearm in a life-and-death situation. Also, if you're buying a chemical spray -- I highly recommend a pepper based spray rated at 1.5 million Scoville heat units (SHU), or better. The other types of sprays have limited shelf-life, and are not always effective.

85. <u>F.S.</u> 790.001(13); <u>L.B. v. State</u>, 681 So.2d 1179 (2DCA 1996).

86. In <u>L.B. v. State</u>, <u>supra</u>, the court held the statute to be vague, and a violation of due process of law.

87. 18 USC 930(g) excludes a pocket knife from the definition of a "dangerous weapon" where the blade lenth is less than 2 ½ inches.

88. 18 USC 930(g)(2)

89. Whether it's a misdemeanor trespass, or a felony depends on whether a self defense pepper spray or nonlethal electric weapon is considered a "dangerous weapon" under <u>F.S.</u> 810.08 & 09. Since a dangerous weapon is one that, taking into account the manner in which it is used, is likely to produce death or great bodily harm — it should be only a misdemeanor. <u>See</u>, <u>Houck v. State</u>, 634 So.2d 180 (5DCA 1994).

90. Opinion of Attorney General, 068-103 (1968)

91. <u>F.S.</u> 790.115(1)

92. <u>Ensor v. State</u>, 403 So.2d 349 (Fla. 1981). <u>Goodman v. State</u>, 689 So.2d 428 (1DCA 1997).

93. <u>F.S.</u> 790.10

94. <u>F.S.</u> 790.115(1)

95. F.S. 790.15

96. An automatic weapon is one which can fire a series of "bursts" (ie: "select fire"), or can fire continuously (automatic mode) -- from a single pull of the trigger.   Such firearms normally have the additional ability to fire single shots in a semi-automatic mode, as well.   The mode on such firearms is controlled by a manually operated switch located on the firearm. A "semi-automatic" weapon is one which is able to reset itself for each succeeding shot, but still requires the trigger to be pulled before each individual shot can be fired.

97. F.S. 790.16

98. See, Rinzler v. Carson, 262 So.2d 661 (Fla. 1972), where the use of a registered submachine gun was condoned in a self-defense situation.

99. F.S. 790.221; 18 USC 5801-5872

100. The definition of a firearm in 27 CFR 179.11 states:

> "The overall length of a weapon made from a shotgun or a rifle is the distance between the extreme ends of the weapon . . . ."

101. F.S. 790.001(9)

102. An "NFA" firearm (but never a "machinegun" or "destructive device") may be placed on the list per 26 USC 5845(a). This is "Section III" of the published list, which then removes the weapon from NFA requirements. However, a machinegun that is a curio, relic, or antique — still needs the Form 4, and tax stamp. Same thing on destructive devices.

103. 26 USC 5845 (e); 27 CFR 179.11

104. Interestingly, a "pistol" is not defined by the statute, but is found only in the regulations, 27 CFR 178.11, although "handgun" is defined in 18 USC 921(a)(29).

105. F.S. 790.151

106. F.S. 790.157(2)(c) makes it "prima facie" that a person is under the influence at 0.10 per cent blood alcohol level. Between 0.05% and

0.10% is a gray area. Below 0.05% — you're presumed to be OK.

107. You might also remember that if you're not sober, you may be too intoxicated to realize you're gun is not really unloaded. Certainly, a sobering thought (no pun intended) to ponder.

108. F.S. 790.19

109. F.S. 790.225

110. A "felony" under Florida law is a crime that could be punished by more than a year imprisonment, regardless of the sentence imposed.

111. F.S. 790.23 & 790.235

112. F.S. 790.23

113. F.S. 790.07(1) & (2)

114. F.S. 775.087(2)

115. F.S. 775.087(3)

116. 18 USC 929

117. F.S. 790.27 & 18 USC 922(k)

118. F.S. 790.27

119. F.S. 790.001(4); 26 USC 5845 (f)

120. A 12 gauge shotgun has a bore more than one half inch.

121. 15 USC 1241-1245

122. 18 USC 921 (30-(31); 18 USC 922 (v)-(w); enacted September 13, 1994.

123. F.S. 370.08; and Fla. Admin. Code 46-4.012(1).

124. IRS Rev. Rul. 55-569.

125. F.S. 810.08 & 810.09

126. F.S. 493.6120

127. 18 USC 922 (x)

128. F.S. 790.17

129. F.S. 790.18

130. F.S. 790.174(3)

131. F.S. 790.174; & the 1997 amendment (C.97-234) to 790.115(2)(c)(2). See also, F.S. 790.175

132. This particular section is governed under the culpable negligence statute, Florida Statute 784.05(3), rather than the chapter on weapons and firearms, Chapter 790.

133. Chapter 97-72, Florida Statutes (1997), and 99-284 in 1999.

134. F.S. 790.33 wisely preempted firearms and ammunition laws (not other weapons) from local governments. However, local government is still restricted on weapons if they pass laws that conflict with C. 790. See, Rinzler v. Carson, 262 So.2d 661,668 (Fla. 1972).

135. K-Mart v. Kitchen, 662 So.2d 977 (4DCA 1995) was reversed by the Florida Supreme Court on July 17, 1997 in Kitchen v. K-Mart (1997 Fla. Lexis 1052), which sustained the jury verdict. Also, in Wal-Mart v. Coker, 22 FLW 1561 (1DCA 6/97), Wal-Mart was found liable for the death of a person when it sold handgun ammo to a minor who then used it to shoot the decedent. Big bucks!

136. F.S. 790.18

137. F.S. 790.225. The real bad news is that federal law can make possession, manufacture, distribution a ten year felony per 15 USC 1245:

> "Whoever in or affecting interstate commerce, within any Territory or possession of the United States, within Indian country (as defined in section 1151 of title 18), or within the special maritime and territorial jurisdiction of the United States (as defined in section 7 of title 18), knowingly possesses, manufactures, sells, or imports a ballistic knife shall be . . .imprisoned not more than ten years. . . ."

138. The answer is obviously not to ban any of these things -- but is to enforce stiff prison sentences against criminals who use guns to commit violent felonies. And that, my friends, also applies to juveniles -- who are literally getting away with murder, because the Legislature still refuses to recognize the threat they pose to all of us, and keeps passing watered-down bills that do little to stop juvenile violence.

139. Ability to accept should mean that if it can be "readily converted" — then it qualifies. The definitions are in 18 USC 921(a)(30)

140. American Rifleman, "You, Your SKS & The Law", by Michael R. Irwin, May 1994.

141. These are listed in F.S. 776.08.

142. Clemons v. State, 37 So. 647, 649 (Fla. 1904).

143. F.S. 776.012 & 776.013. However, pursuant to F.S. 782.02, deadly force may be justifiable to stop the commission of any felony upon your own person, or to stop the commission of a felony upon or in any dwelling house in which you may be, so long as you did not "unnecessarily kill" the perpetrator by using excessive force, per F.S. 782.11.

144. F.S. 776.08

145. A "deadly weapon" is either an instrument which will **likely** cause death or great bodily harm when used in the ordinary and usual manner contemplated by its design and construction, or an object which is used, or threatened to be used in such a way that it would be **likely** to cause death or great bodily harm. Butler v. State, 602 So.2d 1303 (1DCA 1992). In Dale v. State, 22 FLW 670 (Fla. 10/97) the Supreme Court of Florida held that whether an unloaded BB gun was a deadly weapon was a jury question. This is a rather awful decision that makes little sense, and seems to allow a jury to decide if a weapon is deadly from the perception of the victim, rather than from the standpoint of reality or logic. See also, Mitchell v. State, 1997 Fla. App. Lexis 7870 (2DCA 7/29/97), where the court also held an **unloaded** BB gun could be a deadly weapon.

146. Heston v. State, 484 So.2d 84 (2DCA 1986)

147. Similar to a firearm is a nunchaku, or nun-chuks, which is also considered a deadly weapon. Why? Because "unlike common objects

which may be deadly only because of their use or threatened use, the sole modern use of nunchaku is to cause great bodily harm." R.V. v. State, 497 So.2d 912 (3DCA 1986). On the other hand, in the case of Heston v. State, 484 So.2d 84 (2DCA 1986), the court held that an unloaded crossbow was not a deadly weapon as it could not have inflicted injury upon another person without arrows.

148. F.S. 776.06

149. Even though you have no duty to retreat, I would strongly advise that you make it very clear that you want no part of any physical altercation, no matter what your legal rights are. This is because you want to make sure that it's understood you're not participating in any consensual form of mutual combat, nor are you looking for a fight. These are factors which could turn a police officer, prosecutor, or jury -- against you. So, avoid it if you can, and make it clear that you want no part of it. That way, there will be no doubt that you were the victim.

150. F.S. 776.012 & 776.031.

151. Curtilage is the yard area immediately around your dwelling where that portion of the yard is fenced, has shrubs, or something else that clearly marks the outer perimeter of your property. Hamilton v. State, 645 So.2d 555 (2DCA 1994). If you own several acres of property that are all within a common fence -- it is not curtilage -- that would probably be interpreted as the "open fields" portion of your property. Curtilage generally refers to a more immediate area.

152. A motel room is considered a private dwelling. Turner v. State, 645 So.2d 444 (Fla. 1994).

153. Fredericks v. State, 675 So.2d 989 (1DCA 1996) notes that officers are trained to use deadly force against an attacker with a knife within a distance of 21 feet.

154. Actually, if you are on the curtilage of your dwelling, and it's clearly his intention to commit a felony, or misdemeanor other than trespass -- then he is in the commission of a felony, to wit: a burglary. Compare, Baker v. State, 622 So.2d 1333 (1DCA 1993), with Holsworth v. State, 522 So.2d 348, 353 (Fla. 1988); Williams v. State, 504 So.2d 392 (Fla. 1987). At this point, you technically may threaten to use a deadly weapon -- but whether you can actually use it to inflict physical harm will always depend on whether your use was "excessive", or not, under the circumstances.   Moreover, if you display it, and that doesn't dissuade him -- you may be forced into the situation you wanted to avoid in the first place. So, the best advise is always going to be that unless it's a situation where death or great bodily harm is going to result -- use of a deadly weapon by a private citizen is probably not worth the possible civil and criminal repercussions, even if it would otherwise be legal. This advise also applies to the display of such a weapon. Also, remember that the firing of a "warning shot" will always constitute the use of deadly physical force, even if fired into the air or the ground. Miller v. State, 613 So.2d 530 (3DCA 1993). I doubt that this would ever be considered "excessive force" if you were preventing a felony, and if nobody was injured -- but it's not something to be taken lightly. Plus, if you fire it into the air -- the bullet has to come down somewhere!

155. F.S. 776.07(1)

156. F.S. 782.07, and 782.11

157. If the guy definitely has a gun in hand, a warning may not be the safest thing you could do since he could turn, and shoot you, or a bystander, before you could shoot him. While I'm not saying you should shoot first under these conditions -- it's a very tough judgment call.

158. F.S. 784.011 and 784.0211

159. For instance: an injunction against violence; maybe hiring an off-duty police officer to catch the jerk in the act and arrest him (alot cheaper than spending ten grand on me to defend you); etc. There are lots of ways, if you take the time to think about it.

160. F.S. 782.03

161. Florida Standard Jury Instructions, 603 So.2d 1175 (Fla. 1992). See also, Falco v. State, 407 So.2d 203 (Fla. 1981); and Cobb v. State, 376 So.2d 230 (Fla. 1979), where the Florida Supreme Court stated:

> "Homicides committed while resisting anothers unlawful act are punishable only if not excusable, as provided in section 782.03 . . . or if not justifiable, as provided in section 782.02, or chapter 776, Florida Statutes".

162. <u>F.S.</u> 782.03

163. <u>Florida Standard Jury Instructions</u>, 603 So.2d 1175 (Fla. 1992).

164. <u>Prudential Property & Casualty Ins. Co. v. Swindal</u>, 622 So.2d 467 (Fla. 1993).

165. <u>State Farm v. Marshall</u>, 554 So.2d 504 (Fla. 1989)

166. <u>Stewart v. State</u>, 672 So.2d 865 (2DCA 1996)

167. If he was armed -- tell the officer what he had, and where it is now. Hopefully, it does not have your fingerprints on it. More hopefully, it has <u>somebody's</u> fingerprints on it, because if you've wiped it clean, you've tampered with evidence, and screwed your whole case.

168. The Orlando Sentinel, May 7, 1995, Metro Section, editorial by Charley Reese.

ADDENDUM

The addendum to the book is a collection of miscellaneous information which I feel you may find interesting. I strongly suggest you also search the internet for information using search terms such as firearms, weapons, "second amendment". Some excellent websites include: www.gunowners.org (GOA site); www.nra.org (NRA site); www.amfire.org (AFI site); www.ccrkba.org (Second Amend.).

PRIOR EDITIONS OF "FLORIDA FIREARMS":

If you own either of the first three editions (the red or blue books), they are substantially out of date, and **dangerous**. Throw it away, or keep it as a curio. I'm not kidding -- too many things have changed. You should not be using it. I also strongly suggest replacement of the earlier printings of the fourth edition (green book) with a print date **earlier** than December 1998. You can find the printing date at the top of the page immediately before the Table of Contents. The last, and most current printing of the Fourth Edition is still up-to-date, but will need "updates" issued from January 2000, and on. This is the final print run of the Fourth Edition, and will show a printing date of **October 1999.** The Fourth Edition which bears a printing date of December 1998 is current enough not to be "dangerous" — but without the updates — there have still been some major changes which could land you in trouble. Unfortunately, we do not keep old updates in stock. Once a new update comes out — you're out of luck — we can't supply you with an older one. As a practical matter — that means you should probably buy a new book, assuming you really want to know what's going on, and what to be aware of.

UPDATING SERVICE:

I also highly recommend that you send in for the twice yearly cumulative updates. One will be printed in January of each year, and one in August. They cost a one dollar and six cents (**$1.06**) a piece, and you **must** include a **self-addressed stamped envelope**, along with your check. Whenever you send it in, you'll get the most current update printed as we don't hold orders, or take orders for future releases. Please bear with our stupid rules, it makes life bearable for us. We don't print these updates for a profit. They are solely for your benefit.

Updates generally run no more than a page in length, but they do update you to major changes in the law. If you don't care if the law changes — don't send in for them.

LIST OF PRO-SECOND AMENDMENT ORGANIZATIONS:

Should you be interested in protecting your firearm and self-defense rights, here are some of the primary organizations to consider joining. Your membership is important from a standpoint of numbers, and also from a financial standpoint:

National Rifle Association: The most influential of all firearm groups with extensive publications, activities, and political lobbying. Has the best magazine publications out there. Well worth the membership for the subscription, alone. For all information phone: 1-800-672-3888. (dues $35.00 yearly). Join on the web at www.nra.org.

Gun Owners of America: Not as large as the NRA, but extremely active politically, especially at a grass-roots level. Takes an aggressive stand on firearms issues. May have a greater impact on Congress than even the NRA, although that's arguable. Newsletter, e-mail updates, automatic contact with Congress through its Web site, and other programs. Full membership starts at $20.00 yearly. Essential to belong to. Will keep you advised of everything going on in Congress like nobody else can. Main number: (703) 321-8585. To sign-up for membership with credit card phone: 1-800-886-8852. Join on the web at www.gunowners.org

Unified Sportsmen of Florida: This is the Florida State affiliate of the NRA, and is a vital organization for all Florida citizens to belong to. Lobbying of the Florida Legislature, and numerous newsletters advising members of current bills, and happenings. Main phone number: (904) 222-9518. You may join by phoning, and using credit card.

Second Amendment Foundation: Another organization that sponsor's many court cases on firearm issues, and holds activist seminars. Suggested dues are $15.00 or $30.00 -- whichever you can spare. It's well worth supporting. Phone: (206) 454-7012.

INDEX

"G" license 102
1000 feet 8, 55, 85, 87, 113, 114, 117
18 inches 88
26 inches 88
911 . . . . 169, 172, 173

administrative audit 124
Adolph Hitler 140
age of majority 15
aggravated assault 27, 95, 147, 150,
159, 160, 165, 170, 179
airgun 108, 109, 128
airline terminal 56
airport 56, 57, 73, 74, 82, 131
alien 23, 31, 125
antique firearm 14, 94, 135
any other weapon 49, 75, 86, 89, 90,
100, 128
apartment 65, 75, 76
appeal procedure 37
armed trespass 101
armor-piercing 103
assault weapon 100, 133-135, 137
ATF 21, 38, 46, 47, 90, 122-126, 130,
131, 140, 141
ATF Director 47
athletic event 56
automatic firearm 88
automobile 72
ax handle 149

Bahamas 73
ballistic knife 131
bangstick 100
bank 56, 117
bar 27, 46, 56, 84, 137

baseball bat 148, 149, 151, 155

BATF 25, 42, 90, 97, 122, 125, 132,
                                                         141
BB gun 17, 107, 110, 148
bicycle 66
Bill of Rights 1, 2, 4, 7
blood alcohol 92
bound volume 126
bowie knife 16, 19, 128
box cutter 114, 115
Brady Bill 33, 39, 126
brass knuckles 16, 128, 130
bulletproof vest 95
Bureau of Alcohol, Tobacco, and Firearms 25, 46, 122
bus stop 55, 83, 85, 87, 114, 115, 117
buses 74, 75, 84, 86, 109
business premises 77, 81, 124, 125,
                                                    132, 155

castle doctrine 77, 153
cellular phones 172, 173
checks and balances 9, 10
chemical spray 68, 82, 116
civil liability 19, 28, 102, 145, 158, 163
Class III 88
Clemency Board 45
collector 122
college 22, 52, 54-56
Commerce Clause 9, 11
commercial aircraft 73
common area 75, 76
common pocket knife 61, 82
concealed carry 61-63
concealed weapons permit 12, 22, 26,
                        30, 34, 39, 49, 50, 53, 57, 58, 63,
                        68, 70, 74, 75, 81, 91, 102, 126
conditional approval 34-36
conditional approval number 35, 36

conditional pardon 41, 42
condominium 65, 68, 75
console 60, 67, 69, 72, 112
Constitutional Convention 1-3
constructive possession 94
conveyance 65, 66, 70, 71, 73, 101,
                                                                            179
convicted felon 26, 50, 93, 94
criminal history 12, 26, 29, 30, 34, 37,
                                                                          38
Criminal Justice Standards & Training Commission 52, 53
crossbow 85, 94, 148
culpable negligence 111, 112, 158,
                                                                       161, 162
curio 89, 90, 122, 144, 202
curtilage 76, 153, 156

dagger 16
dangerous crime 31, 35
dangerous weapon 15, 84, 150, 161-
                                                                         163
deadly force 85, 88, 147, 149-153, 156-
                                                              158, 165-167, 170
deadly weapon 15, 16, 25, 83, 145-
                                                   149, 151, 156, 159, 165, 166,
                                                                       170
definition of a firearm 13-15, 88, 141
deposition 184
derringer 90, 118
destructive device 14, 98, 99, 114,
                                            115, 130, 131, 147, 159, 179
dirk 16, 128
discharging firearms 87
discharging machineguns 87
dishonorably discharged 24, 47
domestic violence 25, 27, 29, 31, 35,
                                            38, 50, 51, 58, 60, 61, 154
dual residence 22
DUI 28, 50, 59, 91, 92

dummy grenade 130
dummy shell 93, 130
duty to retreat 151, 153, 154
electric weapon 16-18, 55, 82, 84, 86,
93, 107, 108, 114, 115
employee 55, 65, 77, 122, 123
escape 14, 95, 153, 156-158, 163, 170,
181
excessive force 147, 151, 156-158,
163, 165
excusable homicide 161-163, 166
executive clemency 41, 43, 45-47, 50,
93
exploding bullet 97

facility 54
faculty member 55
FDLE 21, 26, 27, 29, 33-39, 51, 59
federal office 56
FFL 97, 121-124, 128, 131, 132
fingerprint 37, 38, 53
fishing, camping, or lawful hunting
. . . . 64
fixed ammunition 14, 89, 137
Florida Constitution 4, 12, 15, 41, 78,
125, 126
Florida Department of Law Enforcemen
t26
folding stock 88, 137, 138, 144
forcible felonies 147, 150, 179
forcible felony 146, 147, 152, 153, 156,
163-166, 169, 179
Founding Fathers 9, 10, 12

Gary Kleck 7, 178
glove compartment 67, 69, 72, 173,
181
GOA 140, 202
grandfathered 143

great bodily harm 15, 16, 84, 92, 146,
148, 149, 152-154, 156, 165-167,
179
Gun Control Act 22, 28, 123

gun shows 12, 30, 90, 112, 126, 129-
131
Gun-Free School Zones 8

hazardous materials 74
Hell Fire 88
high capacity clip 95
hoax bomb 131
holster 66, 67, 69, 70, 75, 90
home 8, 17, 21, 22, 27, 30, 51, 57, 65,
75-77, 81, 107, 109, 122, 132,
133, 147, 153-155, 164, 172, 177,
180
Homeowners Insurance 152, 164
honorable discharge 52
hunting 17, 64, 69, 75, 78, 79, 83, 87,
96, 105, 107, 109, 114, 125, 138,
162
hunting accident 162

imminent 148, 150, 152, 153, 159, 160
improper exhibition 86, 87, 150, 165
injunction 27, 58, 60, 160
instructors 52, 132
insurance 152, 164
international waters 73
interstate commerce 9-11, 131
interstate or foreign commerce 9
intimate partner 24
intoxicated person 127
inventory 124, 126, 132, 134

Justice Brandeis 30
large capacity ammunition feeding device 134

lawful age 105
lead 95, 97, 140, 157, 172
legal disability 16, 23, 29, 35, 41, 42,
                                                                    100, 106
licensed collectors 122
longgun 19, 21, 22, 128
mace 18, 54, 61, 74, 85, 150, 151, 158
machinegun 54, 88, 89, 91, 98, 100
mail 57, 64, 79, 80, 123, 182, 203
mandatory minimum 88, 93-95, 159
manslaughter 27, 112, 147, 157-159,
                                                                    161, 162
manual possession 65, 75
marijuana 24, 127
measure the length 89
mental defective 24, 31, 47
mentally incompetent 35
metal pipe 149
militia 1-3
minor 15, 17-19, 107, 108, 111, 113,
                                                                    127-130
modifications 141, 144
Molotov cocktail 98
multiple firearms 126

National Firearms Act 88, 89, 98
National Forest 78
National Guard 2, 64, 134
negligent 111, 112, 127
next business day 36
NFA 88, 89, 101, 141
NICS 30, 38, 39, 127
Ninth Amendment 8
no firearms permitted 101
noncriminal violation 57
nonlethal electric weapon 84
normal faculties 50, 59, 91, 92

not readily accessible for immediate us 65, 66, 70

NRA 6, 51, 52, 73, 118, 132, 140, 141,
                                                    202-204
nunchaku 148

Office of Munitions Control 23, 125
on or about your person 60
open carry 63, 71, 84-86
openly carry 85
pardon 41-43, 46, 58
pardon power 41
parents permission 16, 19
Parole Commission 45
pawnbrokers 126
pepper based spray 82
pepper spray 55, 82, 84, 117, 168
personal collection 25, 121, 126
place of business 65, 122, 130
pocketknife 16, 68, 83, 107, 110, 115,
                                                    128
police officers 30, 51, 60, 63, 86, 157,
                                                    172, 176, 185
potato cannon 14, 99
powerhead 100
preemption 5, 6
private aircraft 63, 74
private boats 63, 73
probation 28, 29, 31, 35, 43, 47, 51, 53,
                                                    94, 180
prohibited places 53
public transportation 74
pyrotechnic devices 15

razor 114, 115
readily accessible 65, 66, 70, 111, 115,
                                                    117
readily convertible 13, 15
reasonable person 111
reasonably believe 148, 152, 153, 157
reciprocity 61

Regional Director 123
registered student 55
relic 89, 90, 122, 144
Request for Waiver 45
restaurant 56
restoration of civil rights 41-46
restraining order 31, 155
retained rights 7
retreat 76, 77, 151, 153-156
retreat rule 76, 77, 153-155
revocation of your permit 58
Right to Bear Arms 1
school bus 55, 83-87, 109, 114, 115,
                                                   117
school bus stop 55, 83, 85, 87, 114,
                                               115, 117
school property 108, 114-117
school sponsored 109, 114, 115
school zone 8, 114, 117
schools 10, 11, 78, 84, 86, 87, 109,
                                                   115
scienter 82
Second Amendment 1, 2, 6, 133, 140,
                                              141, 203
securely encased 65-67, 70, 74, 75,
                                79, 99, 115, 117, 174
security personnel 102
select fire 54, 87, 100
select militia 2
semi-automatic 87, 88, 135, 136
serial number 98, 100, 134
shoulder stock 89, 128
silencer 13, 89
SKS 97, 141, 143, 144
slungshot 16, 130
spring knife 93, 131
Standard Jury Instruction 152
standing armies 1
starter pistols 15

state parks 79, 100
sterile area 56, 74
switchblade knife 99

Thomas Jefferson 4, 141
training requirements 51, 53, 102
trains 74
trigger lock 70, 111-113
truncated cone 95

unnecessarily 147, 159
UPS 79, 80
use of force 145, 150, 152, 157, 166
vocational school 115
waiting period 12, 26, 29, 30, 39, 44,
                                                               125, 126
waiver 42, 45, 125
warning shot 156, 179, 180
well regulated militia 1-3
willful 54, 57, 85
willfully 17, 20, 55, 57, 107, 108, 112,
                                                                   123
withheld adjudication 24, 29, 35, 50
working hours 34
Youth Handgun Safety 17, 105
Youth Handgun Safety Amendment
      . . . . 17, 105

Federal Statutes:

15 USC 1241 99
15 USC 1245 131
18 USC 921 . . . . 24, 25, 42, 89, 100, 128,
                                                              136, 143
18 USC 921 (a) 42
18 USC 922 . . . . 17, 20, 21, 25, 31, 34, 38,
                                         98, 100, 105, 113, 133, 141-143
18 USC 922 (r) 141, 142
18 USC 922 (v) 100, 133

18 USC 922 (x) 17, 105
18 USC 923(f) 123
18 USC 925 . . . . 46, 141, 144
18 USC 926A 72
18 USC 930 . . . . 54, 56, 83
21 USC 802 24
26 USC 5801 88
26 USC 5845 . . . . 89, 98
26 USC 5871 90
28 USC 1361 123

Federal regulations:
27 CFR 178.11 89
27 CFR 178.39 141
27 CFR 179.11 . . . . 88, 89

Federal forms:
DD214 52
DSP Form 5 . . . . 23, 125
Form 3310.4 . . . . 126, 127
Form 4 89
Form 4473 . . . . 21, 23, 26, 34-37, 39, 126
Form 4498 123
Form 4500 123
Form 4501 123

Florida Statutes:
370.08 100
493.6120 102
741.24 112
741.28 . . . . 25, 27
744.331 50
776.012 . . . . 147, 152
776.013 147
776.031 152
776.06 . . . . 149, 157
776.07 157
776.08 . . . . 146, 147

782.02 . . . . 147, 161
782.03 . . . . 161, 162
782.07 157
782.11 . . . . 147, 157
784.011 159
784.0211 159
784.05(3) 111
790.001 . . . . 14, 66, 70, 83, 88, 98
790.001(15) 70
790.001(16) 66
790.001(9) 88
790.01 . . . . 60, 63
790.05 65
790.052 81
790.053 . . . . 63, 69
790.06 . . . . 52, 54, 55, 57, 59, 82, 115, 132
790.06(1) 54, 57
790.06(12) 54, 55, 82, 115
790.065 . . . . 15, 21, 25, 29, 34
790.065(1) 21, 34
790.065(12) 29, 34
790.065(7) 34
790.09 130
790.10 86
790.115 . . . . 54, 55, 85, 87, 111, 114
790.115(1) 54, 85, 87
790.15 87
790.16 87
790.165 131
790.17 . . . . 16, 18, 107
790.174 . . . . 111, 112, 116
790.175 111
790.18 . . . . 16, 107, 128
790.19 92
790.22 . . . . 17, 107
790.22(3) 17
790.225 . . . . 93, 131
790.23 . . . . 75, 93

790.25 . . . . 63, 67, 69, 71, 74, 76, 77, 99,
                                                                    115, 122
790.25(1) 67
790.25(4) 67
790.27 98
790.28 21
790.31 95
790.33 . . . . 6, 115
810.08 . . . . 84, 101
810.09 101
823.05 57
907.041 27
944.292 41
948.03 28

Florida Constitution:
Florida Constitution 4, 12, 15, 41, 78,
                                                                    125, 126

         Article 1, section 1 7
         Article 4, section 8 41
         Article 8, section 5 12

ORDER
FORM

If you wish to purchase another copy of this book for yourself or a friend, and cannot find it in stores, or do not want to special order it from a book store or on-line vendor such as Amazon.com — then, the reverse side of this page contains an order form for purchases direct from the publisher. We also note that SUBSTANTIAL DISCOUNTS are available on ten or more books purchased at a time by dealers or instructors. If you are interested, please contact the publisher directly at: (407) 650-0770

ORDER FORM & INFORMATION

Although we recommend you purchase through a dealer, instructor, range, bookstore, or on-line service ... additional copies of this edition are available direct from the publisher for price of **$27.77**, which includes tax & shipping. To order by mail, you may pay by money order, cashiers check, or personal check. Sorry, we do not take credit cards. Books are available at many firearm stores, from instructors, Amazon.com, and by "special order" from almost all bookstores (Barnes & Noble, Books-a-Million, etc.) using the ISBN identification number **0-9641958-2-8** which is on the rear cover. We do offer significant discounts to dealers, stores, and instructors, buying ten or more books, and suggest that new dealers call us for discount information before placing their first order.

We <u>cannot ship</u> outside of the continental USA! If you overpay an order, we do not make refunds unless you've got more than two bucks coming to you. This is because our expense on doing a refund runs slightly over two dollars.

Name:	
address:	Apt.
City:	State: Zip:
Phone: ( )	

Check in the amount of $27.77 per book should be made out, and mailed to the following address:

"Jon H. Gutmacher, P.A."
Publishing Division
200 N. Thornton Avenue
Orlando, Fl. 32801
407-650-0770